Defining Moments

*First Lesson Sermons
For Advent/Christmas/Epiphany
Cycle B*

William L. Self

CSS Publishing Company, Inc., Lima, Ohio

DEFINING MOMENTS

Copyright © 1999 by
CSS Publishing Company, Inc.
Lima, Ohio

Library of Congress Cataloging-in-Publication Data

Self, William L.
    Defining moments : first lesson sermons for Advent/Christmas/Epiphany, cycle B / William L. Self.
       p.   cm.
    Includes bibliographical references.
    ISBN 0-7880-1376-9 (pbk. : alk. paper)
    1. Advent sermons. 2. Christmas sermons. 3. Sermons, American. 4. Catholic Church Sermons. 5. Bible. O.T. Sermons.   I. Title.
BV4254.5.S37   1999
252'.61—dc21   99-16007
                                              CIP

This book is available in the following formats, listed by ISBN:
    0-7880-1376-9   Book
    0-7880-1377-7   Disk
    0-7880-1378-5   Sermon Prep

For more information about CSS Publishing Company resources, visit our website at www.csspub.com.

PRINTED IN U.S.A.

To
Carolyn
My One And Only Love

Acknowledgments

I am deeply indebted to many who have helped along the way, most especially to Barbara Brown, my secretary, who has researched, edited, typed, badgered me, and pushed this process along. Now some peace can return to my study. Also to Carolyn who writes along with me, patiently turning scribbled ideas into coherent paragraphs. She, in all areas of my life, continually brings order out of chaos.

Table Of Contents

Introduction

It was over a half century ago, while a student studying for the ministry at Stetson University in Deland, Florida, that I was invited to preach at the prestigious Central Baptist Church in Miami, Florida. Central was at that time the largest and most influential church in the state, and I was honored to be invited to stand in that pulpit. To be honest, I was scared. The service was to be geared to young people and so I accepted the invitation.

The pastor was the greatly loved Dr. C. Roy Angel, who had been there for decades and had greatly influenced the lives of several generations of Floridians and Baptists.

As a young boy living in South Florida, I had listened to the radio broadcast of Dr. Angel preaching as I ate breakfast with my mother before going to Sunday School and "preaching" at my home church fifty miles north at Delray Beach.

Standing in this great man's pulpit was overwhelming. When I arrived at the church on that Sunday morning, a deacon making small talk with me told me of their difficulty with Dr. Angel. It seemed that often on Sunday morning Dr. Angel had to be persuaded to leave his study and enter the pulpit. They often had to dispatch a deacon to help him gather up the courage to preach. Quite frankly, I could not understand this because he had always seemed so masterful and in charge and perfectly at home in the pulpit.

At the time, I did not understand the burden of preaching. It was hard work, but there was a certain liberating confirmation that came with it that made the work worthwhile. Now, after five decades of preaching and four churches later, I fully understand. It's like opening up your soul and letting the people feed on you. It is more than sharing your last best idea — there is something at stake in preaching that exists nowhere else.

7

For years I have enjoyed speaking on the banquet and motivational circuit with corporations and business associations. I have been able to do this along with my church responsibilities. There are many reasons I did it, but the major one is that it is pure delight. You fly into a city and are met by people who feel privileged to escort "the speaker" to the event. The audience is usually of a single profession with a focused objective, highly educated in this specialty, and within the same general age bracket. Their needs are the same, and my job is to communicate, entertain, and motivate. The speech is usually one I have used before, with some variations, and I feel confident that it will do the job. When it is over, they are gracious, generous, and we part at the airport, usually never to see each other again. I have a feeling of exhilaration and contentment. Not so with preaching.

These are the people whose souls God has entrusted to my care. The subject matter I use is life-changing and challenging. It is new material, and on top of that I suffer from overexposure to them because I am their shepherd. I fully understand why Luther collapsed when serving his first Mass because of the spiritual implications of handling the actual body and blood of our Lord. I share with him this feeling that "the preaching of the word of God *is* the word of God." It is a formidable weight, a heavy burden to serve Living Bread to God's people from the pulpit, and if taken seriously, demands our best. After speaking on the circuit I feel pumped; after preaching the word of God to starving people I feel exhausted. Let me hasten to say that I preach because he called me to do it. One cannot do this work otherwise.

Although I have never hidden in my study before a sermon (occasionally I've wanted to *after* I have preached), after five decades of preaching, I fully understand. Preaching is a messy and awesome task. It is not as well-ordered and neat as a lesson in school or a salesman's presentation. The chaos of congregational life — death, rebellion, depression, and the crisis of meetings and holding the institution together — make it messy. The parish minister also has the pressure of the slick television preachers, many times with questionable theology, who have choreographed worship smoothed beyond imagination, setting the benchmark for his people. Most of our people have seen this while they are eating breakfast or shaving on Sunday morning and enter our doors with this in mind, only to be confronted with empty pews, rebellious organists, and off-key sopranos. The parish minister also may have spent most of Saturday night at the emergency room of the hospital with a family whose teenager has been in a near-fatal automobile crash. Or he had to choose between his own son's baseball game or having two more needed hours in the study.

He/she does love the people, walks with them, and possesses the mental firepower to do the job, but being pastor, preacher, and holding it all together makes preaching an impossible task. I really think that this is the best recommendation for a sermon: does it come from the life of the community, does it have the fingerprints of congregational life on it, does it sink a shaft deep into the biblical revelation, and does it communicate?

I have a sign in my study that says quite simply and to the point: "It's Communication, Stupid!" I hope I have exorcised the ghost of the seminary professor that haunts us all while we are preparing and preaching. That ghost calls us to prepare a paper for the faculty, one publishable by an academic press, when what the people need is a message from God's word for human need. The mother deserted by an alcoholic husband, or the parents who have just been informed by their college son that he has come out of the closet and acknowledged himself to be gay — they need a message from God's word in their need.

For too long preachers have examined the ancient texts with tweezers and under strong light as though they are performing an autopsy and as though objectivity and scientific clarity were the goal. These are the words of *life* and they are to be liberated from the page and allowed to roam the hearts of the congregation, bringing help, love, and hope as needed in each situation. Preaching, worship, God's word, and human need are all a mystery, but when mixed together and allowed to ferment, they provide a life-changing explosion. Sermons are not much good if they are free-floating, with no anchor to the life needs of the congregation.

Also, sermons are for the ear, not the eye. There is a great gulf fixed between the two. I have prepared these sermons with the eye

9

in mind, fully aware that they must ultimately be translated into a form that will fit the ear on a Sunday morning.

Winston Churchill, after losing his bid for re-election after World War II, was uncertain of his future. When asked if he might be persuaded to put his remarkable oratory skills to work as a gospel preacher, he quickly replied, "Only a fool believes he can address the same crowd week after week with essentially the same message and continue to hold their attention. I may have lost an election, but I am not a fool."[1] Enough said!

---

1. Edited by Richard Alan Bodey and Robert Leslie Holmes, *Come to the Banquet* (Grand Rapids: Baker Books, 1998), p. 9.

The Waiting Place

Isaiah 64:1-9

While we were keeping our eighteen-month-old grandson for the weekend so his parents could catch up on their sleep, my wife Carolyn and I were talking about this sermon. I had the idea, but it lacked something. Carolyn had taken Benjamin upstairs for his nap. About fifteen minutes later, she came bursting into my study and said, "I've got it! Read this," and she thrust into my hand *Oh, the Places You'll Go!* by Dr. Seuss. As she was reading this book to Benjamin, she came upon these words:

> *The Waiting Place*
> ... *for people just waiting.*
> *Waiting for a train to go*
> *or a bus to come, or a plane to go*
> *or the mail to come,*
> *or the rain to go*
> *or the phone to ring, or the snow to snow*
> *or waiting around for a Yes or No....*[1]

It is Advent, and we are people, pregnant. Pregnant and waiting. We long for the God/man to be born, and this waiting is hard. Our whole life is spent, one way or another, in waiting. Information puts us on hold and fills our waiting with thin, irritating music. Our order hasn't come in yet. The elevator must be stuck. Our spouse is late. Will the snow ever melt, the rain ever stop, the paint ever dry? Will anyone ever understand? Will I ever change? Life is a series of hopes, and waiting, and half-fulfillments. With grace

11

and increasing patience and understanding of this human condition of constantly unsatisfied desire, we wait on our incompleted salvation. "Advent ... invites us to understand with a new patience that very difficult state of being, Advent."[2]

Advent is the waiting place. All of us have been called to spend more time than we want to in the waiting place. The children of Israel were caught there as slaves in Egypt for an impossible length of time. They were longing to be set free from Pharaoh's taskmasters. But their freedom would have meant nothing if they had not had the incubation of the long wait. Or fast forward to Moses leading them out of bondage. Instead of being able to go directly from Egypt to the Promised Land, they had to take a detour by way of Sinai and a forty-year trek through the wilderness so they could be hammered into a nation that was strong enough, hearty enough, and hungry enough to overtake the land.

Now they wait again — captives in Babylon, longing for the God of Sinai and the burning bush to tear open the heavens and come down. Three times in Isaiah 64 they demand God's presence to intervene again in history. Three times they acknowledge their failure and its consequences. They confess their unclean condition and their garments being like filthy rags, and that they will fade like a leaf. They finally realize that all strength is in God's hands and they are but clay, and they confess this in our text.

Creative waiting seems to be a part of the plan of God. Jacob waits in Laban's house for the right bride. Job and Habakkuk are no strangers to the waiting place. These two cry out desperately, wanting to know the mind of God in their own situation. The God who works for those who wait for him is almost directly opposite to the idea of God that is current in the late twentieth century. We have seen God as some mountain to be explored or an argument to be understood — something for us to control.

Only a few of us think of a believer as one who waits for God. In the Bible God takes the initiative at a time when it seems like we can only wait. We must wait, as Israel waited in exile. It is like a mother carrying a child in her womb; she waits for the baby to be born. It is like parents waiting for a teenager to become an adult, or a child waiting for Christmas.

12

Ours is not a culture that wants to wait. We have been pushed ever faster in our desire to hurry up by the advances in technology. For instance, from the year Christ died until the year 1900, the fund of available information for people to know doubled one time. From 1900 to 1950, it doubled again. From 1950 to 1960, it doubled, and it has doubled every two years from 1960 to 1990. It will continue to double every six months until the end of this century. This has created an instant culture that is impatient with having to wait for anything or ever being out of control.

Each bombardment has made our culture impatient as well as insensitive. Process, wait, incubate are not a part of our lifestyle. We are *now*, *hurry up*, and *turn on*.

Those who are thirty years old have been bombarded with a hundred times more images than the 55-year-olds. The over-55 generation favor contact with many of the images they see. The thirty-year-olds have been so bombarded they have lost the emotional impact that an image carries. They cannot savor anything. The young devour images like popcorn, wanting even more images and wanting them more quickly. The old savor them as they would appreciate a fine meal.

Whatever technology has done to our culture, the ways of God have not changed. He still says to us, "Be still and know that I am God." Advent tells us to be still, to be sober, and to make ourselves quiet so that we can receive the truth, a truth that we have been culturally conditioned not to receive. Advent is the waiting place. It prepares us for God's greatest event.

Advent is like a hush in a theatre just before the curtain rises. It is like the hazy ring around the winter moon that means the coming of the snow that will turn the night into silver. *Advent* means *coming*, and the promise of Advent is that what is coming is an unimaginable invasion. The mythology of our age has to do with flying saucers and invasions from outer space, and that is unimaginable enough. But what is upon us now is even more so — a close encounter, not of the third kind, but of a different kind altogether. An invasion of holiness. That is what Advent is all about.

While in the waiting place, get quiet and receptive, like a child waiting to hear a bedtime story and the voice of his father. Hear

13

again the story of the creation of the world, of God's great garden, its destruction, and his efforts to start over again. Hear the story build through the lives of the patriarchs, the kings, the prophets, then its explosion on a starry night in Bethlehem as God's new genesis begins. Through Mary and Joseph, a baby and a few shepherds, it all begins anew. When this rolls in upon us, we are seeing the waiting place as a place of incubation, a place of preparation before revelation and proclamation.

Waiting through a cold winter does not prevent the necessary activity preceding growth and development from occurring in the roots of trees and shrubs. Waiting through a pregnancy heightens the preparation for a child to be born. Gestation precedes celebration. Everything worthwhile needs incubation. Nothing worthwhile comes without preparation. Nothing worthwhile is born outside the waiting place.

"The greatest revelation is stillness," said Lao-Tzu, and it is most often in this stillness that we become aware of the Holy Spirit and Jesus. It is in this engraced stillness of Advent that we, after the example of Mary, yield to being God-bearers in the world. In this stillness, we commit to being Christ's presence in the world, the flesh of faith, the unfolding of the incarnation.

God makes this plain: "They who wait for the Lord shall renew their strength" (Isaiah 40:31). "But when the time had fully come, God sent forth his Son ..." (Galatians 4:4). In other words, we had to wait for God to get the world ready. Now, we must wait for God to get us ready.

Thus, we need Advent to make ourselves ready for his coming. We need a season of soberness in a world of Christmas parties. We need Advent, the season of waiting, in a world that says *go for it* and *hurry up*. This waiting place called Advent not only prepares us for the birth of God in the flesh, it prepares each of our lives to receive him.

This waiting place called Advent prepares us for God's surprise and joy, or as Dr. Seuss says it, the next place where "boom bands are playing with banners flip-flapping." This is what it did for Nelson Mandela, who spent 27 years — 10,000 days — as a political prisoner in South Africa. During this waiting time, the revolution was shaping. Discontent with apartheid was brewing in the soul of a country. Twenty-seven years of waiting and wondering, 10,000 nights of loneliness and separation, 27 years of deprivation and humiliation. But in that waiting place strength and focus, vision and determination were forged so that when the apartheid system fell, he emerged to preside over a free nation. "It was during those long and hungry years that my hunger for the freedom of my own people became hunger for the freedom of all people, white and black. I knew as well as I knew anything that the oppressor must be liberated just as surely as the oppressed. When I walked out of prison, I knew my mission to liberate the oppressor and the oppressed."[3]

The waiting place prepares us for the angel chorus announcing his birth. Without the waiting place, our hearts are not sensitive and our appetites are not ready. Welcome to God's waiting place. It is the necessary place of preparation. Christmas is God's response to the cry of our hearts. It is Jesus Christ, God's future, taking hold of our hearts — hearts that have confessed that they are falling leaves before the winter wind, hearts that are now ready to become molded like clay. This could not have happened without the waiting place.

The waiting place changes our eyes. Before the waiting place, Israel saw Babylon as their problem. But during the waiting place, they saw that they were the problem and Babylon was only the setting.

The waiting place changes our hearts and confirms that we can do nothing but get ready. The initiative is in God's hands.

The waiting place confirms that someone somewhere loves us enough to make all things new, and this can begin with us. *What* we wait for determines *how* we wait. It determines life in the meantime.

Recently, *Time* magazine ran a cover story about Billy Graham, "A Christian in Winter, Billy Graham at 75." "While he has learned to number his days," the story says, "Billy Graham intends to make the most of them. 'I don't know why God has allowed me to have this; I'll have to ask when I get to heaven. I think heaven is going to be a wonderful place, beyond anything we can imagine.' "

While we wait, we live toward what we cannot begin to imagine. It's winter now; it's exile now; but what we expect on the other side, God's presence, his revelation, his salvation, determines how we wait. The Christian in winter can wait for God to do what God has promised, knowing that nothing can ever tear us away from the love at work on our behalf. By waiting patiently and being open to the movement and processes of God rather than stubbornly refusing his offer of spirit and vision, we hear the boom bands playing and become receptive to his gifts of himself. We are fully alive in the face of whatever life's situation we may find ourselves. "... No one has heard, no ear has perceived, no eye has seen any God besides you, who acts on behalf of those who wait for him" (Isaiah 64:4).

Henri Nouwen, from an article in *Weavings* titled "Our Waiting," says that all action ends in passion because the response to our action is out of our hands. That is the mystery of work, the mystery of love, the mystery of friendship, the mystery of community — they always involve waiting. And that is the mystery of Jesus' love. God is revealed in Jesus as the one who waits for our response. Precisely in that waiting the intensity of God's love is revealed to us. If God forced us to love, we would not really be lovers.[4]

Will God come upon us in the power of holiness and find us unheedful, acting as if our salvation lies at the mall or in the catalogs or in the frantic face of holiday fever? Or will he come among us and find us actively waiting, open and present to the mystery of all mysteries? Will God find us "paying attention to Jesus," as John the Baptist mentioned, or to the hundreds of lesser lights that dim the reality of the coming light? Will we, in other words, be open to an Advent discipline that is truly preparatory — to experience what the apostle Paul wrote: "For God, who said, 'Let light shine out of darkness,' made his light shine in our hearts to give us the light of the knowledge of the glory of God in the face of Christ" (2 Corinthians 4:6)?

One wonders just where and how the hush in the theatre before the curtain rises finds a place in our lives long enough to listen for the invasion of holiness. How and where does Advent in this sense of still waiting happen to us? How and where do we detach from, as Buechner says, "the mythology of our age"? How do we listen? How do we disengage from the invasion, from our worlds, long enough to see the hazy ring around the winter moon that means the coming snow that will turn the night into silver? Dietrich Bonhoeffer, the martyred Lutheran pastor, while imprisoned by the Nazis, wrote a letter before Christmas 1943, in which he said: "Life in a prison cell reminds me a great deal of Advent. One waits and hopes and putters around but in the end what we do is of little consequence. The door is shut, and it can only be opened from the outside."

We enter the reality Isaiah proclaimed. The glorious new creation is coming. The new heavens and the new earth are coming. "Jerusalem is a delight and its people a joy" (Isaiah 65:18b). God is faithful. The promise he made to our fathers, to Abraham and his children forever, is coming true. Stay awake. Be present. Move to the edge of your seat. The hidden is about to be made manifest. The ultimate exodus is unfolding.

---

1. Dr. Seuss, *Oh, the Places You'll Go!* (New York: Random House, 1990).

2. Gertrud Mueller Nelson, *To Dance with God* (Paulist Press, 1986), p. 61-62, quoted from *Synthesis*, December 19, 1993.

3. Nelson Mandela, *Long Walk to Freedom* (New York: Little, Brown & Company, 1994), p. 64.

4. *Synthesis*, December 23, 1993.

Getting In
Tune Again

Isaiah 40:1-11

A radio station in Missouri had an interesting experience. They had a popular program that played the music that most of us like — music middle-America could understand. The program had a very loyal following. People would stay up into the night to listen. It became their friend, especially to those people who have difficulty sleeping. One day the disc jockey got an interesting letter. It said, "Dear Sir, I am a farmer living alone on my farm. My wife is dead and my children and grandchildren have moved away. I see them infrequently. There are three things in my life that give me comfort. One is the farm. Another is this radio program. The third is my fiddle. Sometimes in the night when you are playing music that I have known in past years, I get out my fiddle and play along with you. It brings me great comfort. But recently, a problem has developed. My fiddle is out of tune. The A string doesn't work like it should, and I don't have a tuning fork so there is no way I can get my fiddle back in tune. Would you be so kind as to play the note A? If you will do this, I will tune my fiddle." So the station did, and he did, and they all lived happily ever after.

Christians and their churches have a tendency to get terribly out of tune. This is reflected in the way that churches conduct their lives. It is tragic when this happens. Sometimes the church becomes a political base rather than an evangelistic force. Sometimes it seeks to substitute coercion for conversion. Sometimes the church debates doctrine night and day, and as great doctrinal debates are going on, we forget that we all see "through a glass darkly." Churches forget that the essential matters of scripture we understand. We know

19

enough to tell the world that they are lost without Jesus Christ. The constant debating of doctrine and redefining orthodoxy will get a church out of tune.

Another evidence of being out of tune is when a church will set limits on the province of God. They will set limits on how far the gospel goes and for whom the gospel is intended. As a pastor, I see this happening all the time. Christians will say, "This is not a part of what God wants us to do." Too many modern Christians forget that God has the whole world in his own heart. It is difficult for us to stay focused all the time because there are so many things that distract us. We have things like weekend sports and business meetings that we elevate to a place of prominence. As we come to the Advent season, we must understand that it is more than a "huggy-touchy-feel good-chestnuts roasting on an open fire" kind of season.

Candidly, I like Christmas. I grew up in a home that didn't make much of Christmas. I married into a family that made everything of Christmas, and I like Christmas. I even like the shopping centers, if I don't have to go very often. I like decorating the house. I get the Christmas lights from the attic, bring them down, and usually spend three days untangling them and at least two more days trying to find a replacement bulb so they will work. Last year when we got the lights down from the attic, they unfolded perfectly. I plugged them in and every light worked. That was a great surprise for us. I have never had that experience in my entire life. I knew right then it would be a good Christmas. Another thing that I like about Christmas is that it forces us to define again who Jesus is in our lives and what his birth means for us and our world. As we do this, we cannot escape the fact that we must focus on getting in tune with his mission for our lives.

I never will forget the time my brother heard me preach for the first time. We had grown up in different cities. He was much older than I and we didn't really know each other. After graduation from seminary, I was pastor of a church in North Carolina, and my brother came to worship with us. He spent the weekend in our home, and on the way to church he said, "Bill, I have never heard you preach. What are you preaching today?" I replied, "I'm preaching a sermon on missions." He looked at me and said, "You mean I have driven all the way across the state of North Carolina to hear you preach for the first time, and I'm going to hear a sermon on missions?" It was a downer for him. I don't know if the sermon was good or bad, but I do know one thing — that is the way many Christians see the mission of the church — as extra baggage. Mission sermons somehow rate right in there with stewardship sermons. Perhaps that is why we are out of tune. We forget that the Bible has a global view. Isaiah 40:1-5 talks about the people who have been in darkness having seen a great light. Isaiah, the great prophet of the exile, focuses in and says, "And the glory of the Lord shall be revealed, and all mankind together will see it." God never has intended for his boundaries to be set any less than the whole world. The Bible wants the providence of God to be for the whole world. Don't forget the book of Jonah. Jonah, the man who was running from God, thought that if he could get out of Israel, he would be free of God. So he was going to go as far west as he could in order to get away from him. He got to the shore of the Mediterranean, bought passage on a ship thinking, "I'll leave God in Israel," but God followed him even into the belly of a specially-created sea monster. So he repented, was delivered, and started to go east, not really believing God could go across the Jordan River, and God followed him even to the pagan city of Nineveh and did a mighty work in the hearts of the Ninevites. God is not as narrow as we make him. The New Testament is the same way. This God is for the whole world.

The New Testament says repeatedly that God pushes boundaries back. Israel was there to bear witness to God's purpose, but so was the New Testament church. Paul makes it very clear in all his letters that the gospel is for the entire world. Any church that lives and thrives and survives must have a global view. Any church that is getting ready to die shrinks its boundaries and says, "It's just for us; it is for our little group." Those who define the ministry of the people of God as only being a "feel-good ministry" and who "dumb it down" only take care of the needs of those few who are assembled there. A church focused on itself only is conducting an "ensmallment" campaign.

21

We see this clearly in two churches in the New Testament. One is the church in Jerusalem. At Pentecost 3,000 people were added. That is a good start for a new church. But they got out of tune with a debate over how they would fit with Judaism. The church in Jerusalem was masterful at procedure. They had, for the most part, come out of Judaism and were trying to make this new religion as much like Judaism as possible. Compare this to the church in Antioch, the northern city. That church may not have had all of its procedure down but it had its vision right, and vision gives life. Procedure gives death. The Antioch church decided that it was for the world, and it was going to do something no one had ever done. They were going to send out some people who were to be missionaries and establish new churches: Paul and Barnabas, and then later Paul and Silas. Everywhere Paul went, they were poorly received. They were stoned, beaten, and thrown into prison. However, when it was over, the church had been established. Later they went into Europe. When you go to Israel, you cannot find the site of the church in Jerusalem. In Antioch, on the side of a hill, the site of that great church with its altar still stands as a tribute to their vision. They were in tune.

It is a matter of life or death. Contract and pull in, build a high wall, and you will get out of tune. The church is nothing more or less than a fellowship of witnesses. "It is wholly possible to have a religion without the missionary thrust. When this occurs, the religion goes on as a cultus chiefly directed to the welfare of its constituents or communicants. Without much difficulty, people can be satisfied with their own peace of mind or cultivation of their own spirits. There can be emphasis upon worship and ceremony, with a priesthood and a valued ritual. In a real sense people who participate in such religion tend to their own business and do not bother others. They can continue in this vein, devoid of mission, and maintain good relations even with an atheistic or dictatorial governmental régime."[1]

The church of Jesus Christ does not have a mission; its very life is mission. As a fire does not have heat, its life is heat, and it burns. We need to understand that it is wholly possible to have a religious organization and not have a missionary thrust, but it is out of tune.

How do we get ourselves in tune? We must remember who we are. Any church who does not understand that it has a big horizon is asking for death, and there never has been a narrower work for the church than the whole world. It was the *world* God so loved. Whatever sails on a lesser sea is not the ark of salvation, nor does it belong in the Christian fleet. Why does our violin get out of tune? Maybe we have received a confused message.

How do we tune our fiddles? The gospel is the A note. Get your fiddles and let's tune them now.

I want to tell you a series of stories that have helped keep me in tune. There was a deacon in a church I served who did not believe in doing mission work. He lived in the "objective mood" and the "kickative case." He disagreed with everything that happened. He was a standard-issue church type — he stood around and smoked before church; he wore a big wide tie purchased in 1946 when he got out of the army; he never agreed with anybody on anything. I think he was the belt-over-the-stomach, not the belt-under-the-stomach, type. He never came into the service until the second hymn. The women and children had to be in first, then he would come in. He was the male equivalent to the Church Lady on *Saturday Night Live*. He never said anything that didn't sound like it was written in old English script. One day he accosted me after a mission sermon and said, "Look at all the money we wasted in China." I asked him what he meant. He said, "The Communists have taken over and we spent all that money on mission work and now the churches are out of business. We wasted all that money in China." He always said that before and after the mission sermon. This gave me a lot of encouragement as I went in to preach. Every year it was a ritual. "Look at all that money we wasted in China." We would get ready to approve the budget and he would stand and oppose the whole mission section. "Look at all that money we wasted in China." The whole church could do it as a litany. They knew what this man was going to say. When I did his funeral, I wanted to say, "Look at all that money we wasted in China."

I recently read again the history of missions in China. Those old pioneer missionaries were a crusty bunch of people. That work started about 1805, and was the centerpiece of the mission appeal in England and the United States for about 150 years. Those tough pioneer missionaries didn't know the language, but they would rent a room, start preaching and teaching, and before long, they had a church. They learned the language and started planting more churches. When their mission societies called them home, they would reply, "No, I don't want to come home." They survived the Boxer Rebellion, a time when the Chinese were killing all foreigners in their country. They endured the Japanese war with China. They endured the Communist persecution. They went underground during the Communist takeover, and the only thing we know about what happened is that when the Communists relented and allowed the Christians to declare themselves, the church had grown. One in every 23 Chinese is a Christian. It is hard to believe. When I read that, I wanted to run down to the cemetery and stand over a grave and say, "Look at all the money we wasted in China." Can you imagine that one in 23 of the world's biggest country is a Christian? Thirty-three million Protestants and eighteen million Catholic Christians are in China![2]

We have taken too small a view of God's work. We think like businesspeople — if we don't have a profit every quarter, it's wrong. God thinks in decades and centuries and millennia. God takes the long view; we take a little view. God works somewhere else, above time. We need to understand that the mission of the church *is* the mission of the church.

Those of you who are young to the faith and for the first time beginning to see the work of the church understand that the faith is more than your neighborhood. It is more than your child being satisfied on a ball team; it is more than you being stroked. For those of you who have been in the faith a long time, it is more than somebody visiting you. If you want to get your violin in tune, see the world.

The old categories of "home" and "foreign" missions are gone now with the reality of jet airplanes, e-mail, computers, and fax machines. Flexible borders exist. You can do foreign mission work in Miami as well as you can do it in South America. In fact, Miami is a South American city, some have said. You can do Asian missions in Chamblee, Georgia, as well as you can do it in Hong Kong or Seoul. We must go where the people are. The gospel teaches that everyone needs the chance to hear the gospel.

What does this mean for you? It means that your life can be in tune only if you get in tune with what God is doing in this world. The dumbest thing I ever did was take a youth choir to Colombia, South America, the drug capital of the world; but it was the smartest thing I ever did too. We went with medical doctors from village to village as they were giving medical help to indigent, native Indian people in Colombia, South America. I have walked back in the jungle in Liberia, West Africa, with two doctors and three native men from the school where I was preaching. We went from village to village. They preached and we were there to observe, but the people observed us also. We had gone through about five villages, gathering the people together, and the young men were preaching from pictures and diagrams. When we got ready to go back, one of the young men said, "Let's pray before we go back." He prayed for all the right things, then said, "Lord, keep the snakes off us." A young man walked in front and one in back with machetes in case snakes got in the way or fell off the trees on us. The point is: the Church, by the proclamation of the Gospel of Jesus Christ, has never taken the comfortable route. It has always been pushing back the barriers. It has never been in the easy places, and it has never been easy for the Church. Our church is only a home base for making sure the gospel is being preached around the world. The gospel is for all people; it is for all flesh. Let's tune our violins.

---

1. Elton Trueblood, *The Validity of the Christian Mission* (New York: Harper & Row, 1972), p. 17.

2. *Christian History*. Vol. XV, No. 4, p. 41.

Will The Real Messiah Please Stand Up?

Isaiah 61:1-4, 8-11

In the early days of television a popular game show, *To Tell the Truth*, held the attention of the American audience. A panel of interesting and colorful experts was in place, along with an engaging host. They were presented with three contestants, each claiming to be a famous person or a person who had accomplished an unusual feat. The identity of the real person was known only to the host. After a period of questioning by the panel when the panel and everyone else had been given a chance to vote for their choice of the real person, the host would call for the identity to be revealed — "Will the real (Swiss mountain climber) please stand up?" After a few seconds of suspense, this person would stand. The audience would gasp and the contestants would be rewarded in accordance with their ability to fool the panel of experts.

Somehow I feel we are being called on to play the game today with the many false messiahs presenting themselves as we approach the twenty-first century. In fact, throughout history, we have always had our false messiahs, from David Koresh and Jim Jones to Nero and Philip of Macedon. Each one in his own style offers a safe civilization to humankind if we would but submit. The problem is that it is difficult to distinguish the false messiahs from the real Messiah. There is a hunger within each of us to say, "Will the real Messiah please stand up?"

I. A closer look at some false messiahs.

The Germans have a saying that sums up the wreckage left to us by the false messiahs: "Whatever men do, it turns out lousy."

They, of all people, should know. The Russians throw out the czars and end up with Stalin. The Americans free the slaves so they can move into the ghettos. The Jews have a bad record at this point also. The nation that God chooses to be the hope of the world becomes the stooge of the world. The nation of priests becomes a nation of international politicians so inept at playing one major power off against another that by the time they are through, Egypt, Syria, Babylonia, Persia, Rome, all have a chance of wiping their feet on them — the cream of the population deported, the Temple destroyed, and Jerusalem razed. To top it off, the law of Moses becomes the legalism of the Pharisees, and "What must I do to inherit eternal life?" becomes "Is it kosher to wear my dentures on the Sabbath?" The high priests sell out to the army of occupation and the Holy City turns into Miami Beach. God gets fed up also and nobody knows all of this better than the Jews themselves. After all, they have a wailing wall. But they went on hoping anyway, and several centuries before the birth of Jesus, much of their hope took the form of an implausible dream that someday God in his fathomless mercy would send them Somebody to make everything right. This Somebody was referred to as the Messiah, the Anointed One, the one and only anointed by God as a king at his coronation is anointed, only for a bigger job. The Greek world for messiah is *Christ*.

How and when the messiah would come was debatable. Theories as to what he would be like multiplied and overlapped. A great warrior king like David, a great priest like Melchizedek, a great prophet like Elijah, who could possibly say? But whoever he was, his name would be called Wonderful Counselor, Mighty God, Everlasting Father, Prince of Peace.

However, any role call of the false messiahs of history will prove that the Germans were right: whatever men do, it turns out lousy.

Arnold Toynbee reminds us that these false messiahs come in all sizes and shapes, and they have not changed our world for the better. The messiahs, as statesman or soldier, teacher or pacifist, have all proven inadequate to change humankind. They have made some difference, but they have failed to make us different.

In America in recent years, we have invented our own false messiahs. We have been duped into thinking that technology will save us, only to find out that every technological breakthrough brings its own brand of evil. Americans also believe, whether they will admit it or not, that in a culture as unstable and as cumbersome and inefficient as democracy, something more solid must be adopted.

As a pastor, I have observed that another false messiah that seems to dominate the life of our people is corporate culture. This seems to have more control over the lives of our people than the gospel they profess. "How my company does it" seems to reign supreme. After all, corporate culture does provide for a good retirement. Corporate leaders talk about their companies being a family, but when it comes time to make a profit, people are treated as though they were disposable cartons to be thrown away, sacrificed to the great god, profit. Obviously, a corporation is not a family. Its goal is not to nurture people, but to make a profit. And if people must be sacrificed to make that profit, then so be it.

Another false messiah in America is big-time athletics. Every parent hopes that big-time athletics will rescue them from the difficulty of paying tuition bills for their young quarterback. Every little league father has a dream of owning his own major league team. Newnan, Georgia, recently had to put security officers at the little league park to keep the parents from fighting with one another. Big-time athletics and its control of our lives start from the first Saturday morning a child shows up to play soccer until the day his health breaks and he cannot buy a ticket to go to the ballpark to watch his favorite team. If you don't believe this, do a study on what happens to the worship habits in a city when major league athletics are introduced. Or try calling into judgment our obsession with the football team at any state university.

II. Marks of the real messiah.

Out of the confusion over these false messiahs, we must ask the question, "Will the real messiah please stand up?" How will we know the real messiah, the genuine article, when he appears?

After all, our record of running after the false ones is pretty dangerous. We know we are in a mess. We need someone to bail us out. We don't want to risk following the wrong one.

The divinely inspired prophet tells us what the messiah will be like. He tells us his distinguishing characteristics, for God wants us to identify him correctly. This savior seems to have three basic characteristics. One, he will have a defined audience, and that audience will have four types of people in it. The first will be the meek. The different translations bounce between poor and meek but the essence for the Hebrew is the same — the afflicted, the oppressed, the helpless, the meek. It is interesting that the Messiah himself later says, "The meek shall inherit the earth." However you translate *meek* you must be certain of the fact that it does include all the young, the old, and the helpless, but it excludes the self-sufficient. After all, they think they don't need a savior.

The second will include the brokenhearted, and who among us doesn't fit that category? The graduates of the school of suffering clearly recall loss, betrayal, disappointment. They carry in their hearts the scars of the wrongs which they have suffered, and even more deeply the wrongs they have done. They are brokenhearted; they cannot receive and they cannot give restitution. The Hebrew here is simply *to break in pieces*. They are like ships broken by the storm or people torn asunder by wild beasts. But we must understand that even in the most disastrous human situations, when sorrow robs the heart of its last resources and strengths, the Bible discovers an opportunity for the coming God. The Lord hears those whose hearts are broken. "A broken and contrite heart, O God, thou wilt not despise." Every kind of human helplessness is a recommendation to God.

The third category of people in this audience will be the captives. The world is full of captives. They are the victims of evil habits and ill-regulated deeds, settling down into an ill-regulated life. It is like Paul describes them in 2 Timothy 3:6: "...with sin, led captive with diverse lust." There are many people who have been enslaved by strange forces in strange situations.

The last are those that are bound. They are essentially those who are prisoners and live in the darkness of the prison house in endless gloom. The Bible has no problem classifying the prisoners and the blind as the same, because they both sit in darkness. This messiah will have in his audience those who are longing for the light and are bound in darkness.

The second characteristic of this messiah will be what he says to this strange audience. He speaks a word of encouragement. It is good tidings to each group or person. The task assigned is simply to bring good tidings to proclaim. The message of the Messiah is not advice or an explanation of current events; it is word of what God has done in the subsequent liberation of the human spirits. Grace is God's constant attitude toward men, and vengeance is an occasional judgment necessary to remove obstacles to the grace. There is always a critical juncture when the good tidings of God are heard. One is either the better or the worse, never the same, after hearing the message. The real messiah brings this message.

What is the third characteristic of the true messiah? The third characteristic of the true messiah is that the spirit of the Lord is upon him. It is hard to discern but it is clear. "He anointed me to preach." False messiahs have the spirit of avarice. False messiahs have the spirit of political power upon them. False messiahs depend upon the structures of this world. The true messiah is dependent upon God alone.

III. The real messiah *does* stand up.

One thousand years later in a ragged little village on the topside of an unimportant country, a young man armed only with the spirit of God declared himself the messiah. This is Mary's boy, the one we have seen in the village market. Why, this is the boy who helped Joseph build my house. How can he be the messiah? He is not the messiah. There is no pomp, no manifesto, no dazzling wealth nor connections in high government circles. Jesus was armed only with the spirit of God upon him and the word of God within him. It is clear that from his humble beginnings and his focus upon ministry, he met the criteria for the Isaiah prophecy. Their response, rushing him out of the synagogue and trying to destroy him at the edge of the city, was the response that all stuffed-shirts and self-sufficient people who do not need this kind of messiah, and who wish to

31

make a messiah in their own image, give. Let's get rid of a messiah who doesn't look like the kind of messiah we expect. Let's destroy a messiah who does not fit our image.

When the real messiah stood up, kingdoms fell and despots shuddered. When the real messiah stood up, the poor received him gladly and the power brokers tried to destroy him. The real messiah has stood up and he calls for us. The messiah has stood up and it has made all the difference. Years later when John the Baptist was in prison and asked for reassurance that Jesus was the messiah, he was told simply to look at the evidence. That same word comes to us: "Look at the evidence."

In a few days we will celebrate the birth of the real messiah. We have waited and prepared for his coming. We can either destroy him, or we can honor and invite him into our hearts. The real messiah has stood up. The challenge is with us. "... a historian without any theological bias whatever cannot portray the pageant of human progress without giving a foremost place to a penniless preacher from Nazareth."[1] The real Messiah *has* stood up.

---

1. Hugh Martin, *Parables of the Gospels* (London: SCM, 1957), p. 91.

The Agenda
Factor

2 Samuel 7:1-11, 16

Architecture and power are Siamese twins joined at
the hip. Rulers have always wanted to translate their power into
brick and mortar — from the tower of Babel and Egypt's pharaohs
to Chairman Mao, Joseph Stalin, and Adolf Hitler. I. M. Pei, in his
contract given by François Mitterand to renovate the Louvre, was
commissioned to re-establish the glory of France. Serious resources
have been committed by rulers to display their strength and gran-
deur with architecture.

David had finally consolidated his kingdom and established
his city on Mount Zion. The cost of this had been enormous and
David's hands were bloody from the fighting and intrigue. Now he
lived in a fine palace with cedar walls on Mount Zion, and Israel, a
nomadic nation of runaway slaves in a tiny crossroads country,
was at least looking respectable in the family of nations. King David
looked like a king and lived like a king. After all, Hiram, king of
Tyre, had made this possible by giving him this beautiful palace.
All's well that ends well. No longer an outlaw, no longer a con-
tender — he was king and looked and lived the part, and he wanted
people to notice. He announced to his private chaplain, Nathan,
that he had great plans for God's house too. Perhaps David felt
guilty about the disparity between his house and God's tent. It could
be that after all of this building for himself, he was beginning to
have buyer's remorse or builder's remorse. Perhaps it was a rainy
night in Jerusalem, and while he was feeling safe and dry in his
great house, he had a pang of conscience as he thought of the ark
of God in a very vulnerable shelter. Could he not hear the flapping

of the tent as the wind blew and the rain descended? "I'll do something for God. I'll build God a house as good as my own," he announced to Nathan. "I live in a palace of cedar, while the ark of God remains in a tent" — very noble indeed.

People who covet power and court it constantly know instinctively that every opportunity to demonstrate the power they possess must be taken. Yes, David lived well but his God did not. Could David be so powerful and his nomadic desert God live in a battered old tent? After all, the other deities in surrounding empires lived well. Could the God of Israel be much at all if his house was so scruffy?

David prepares to build a suitable "house" for God, a temple fitting for the God of a new great nation (or, at least, a wanna-be nation) and a great king (again, a wanna-be king) like David. Nathan agrees; after all, he would be senior minister in the new temple. It sounded good, and in all likelihood would sit well with the people. The only thing wrong with it was that God did not see it that way.

> *That night the word of the Lord came to Nathan, saying: "Go and tell my servant David, 'This is what the Lord says: Are you the one to build me a house to dwell in? I have not dwelt in a house from the day I brought the Israelites up out of Egypt to this day. I have been moving from place to place with a tent as my dwelling' " (vv. 4-6).*

God said to Nathan, "Go and tell David I have always met my people in a tent. That is how I identify myself with them."

The Lord will make you a house (v. 11). If any houses are to be built or dynasties established, God will do it, not David. David did not fool God by this very generous offer to build God a nice house. This was only an extension of David's plan for himself, disguised as a generous thing to do for God. This empire needed a more manageable, predictable deity, but God had no intention of being domesticated by Israel. "What makes you think you are the one to build me a house to live in?" (2 Samuel 7:5). David needs to shore up his power, but God doesn't need it. Yahweh was not been tied down to a building but has always roamed freely, even before he adopted Israel. Why should he be domesticated now? He will operate on God's agenda, not David's. After all, who is the real king here anyway?

The dwelling in a tent motif carries over to the prologue in John's gospel, "The Word became flesh and made his dwelling among us" (John 1:14). God always insists on his own agenda. He will not be domesticated.

This kingdom will not be established on David's agenda with his public works program. God has an agenda and he will establish the house of Israel forever, longer and beyond the life of a temple. He will do it his way and in his own time frame, and better than anyone could imagine.

Indeed, the agenda factor is the real issue for most of us. At first glimpse, it appears that God would be a great enhancement for living. Doesn't he part the seas and send the manna? With Jesus many followed at the beginning because he could heal them, feed them, raise them from the dead. Not a bad deal, Hosannah! This taking-up-the-cross stuff should be negotiated out. Sacrifice and the second mile sounds good but it is not to be taken very seriously.

This agenda issue goes to church with the modern Christian also. Garry Trudeau, the creator of the *Doonesbury* cartoon, portrays a character and his wife looking for a church. As they interview the pastor of the Little Church of Walden, they ask if the church has a volleyball team. The pastor replies, "No." The couple then exclaims, "And you call yourself a church?"

Most pastors have been through this ordeal, having to answer questions from people "shopping" for churches that meet their agendas. As Trudeau expresses in another cartoon, a questioning couple is talking with the pastor, and they say, "Doesn't the task of redemption imply guilt?" The pastor answers, "Well, yes, I do rely on the occasional disincentive to keep the flock from going astray. Guilt's part of that!" The next panel shows the inquiring couple responding, "I don't know. There is so much negativity in the world as it is...." She says, "That's right. We're looking for a church that's supportive, a place where we can feel good about ourselves. I'm not sure the guilt thing works for us." He replies, "On the other hand, you *do* offer racquetball." She says, "So did the Unitarians, Honey. Let's shop around some more."

Too many see the Christian life as expressed in the church as the "Good Ship Lollipop." You remember the film, or have seen it in an old movie on television: Shirley Temple dancing joyfully with Bo Jangles on the deck of the Good Ship Lollipop, which is filled with happy people, cared for by a helpful captain and crew who are no more than social directors dedicated to the happiness, entertainment, and indulgence of the passengers. Occasionally, the Good Ship Lollipop as a church gets hijacked by those on board who see its primary purpose as political or social — either way, they impose their own agendas on the old ship of faith. Others use the Good Ship Lollipop as a means to advance their careers, or otherwise force it to serve their private agendas. And the ship loses its way as well as its purpose for being.

The agenda factor is clear in the old story of the lifesaving station on the coast of Maine. The lifesaving crew was known for the efficiency with which they were able to pull out of the raging surf those whose ship had been torn apart by the rocks along the coast. The lifesaving crews were well disciplined and effectively trained. They took justifiable pride in the way they rescued people from the raging surf. As success came their way, they bought uniforms, built a clubhouse, held parties and other social gatherings, and in every way enjoyed their volunteer work.

They became so absorbed in supporting the work of the lifesaving station that some began to feel that going into the surf to rescue those who were drowning was an imposition. After all, they had to attend to the affairs of the club. So others were hired to do the work of lifesaving so that the original crew could support the work of the club, or foster other work that had presented itself. Finally, after one particularly devastating storm, the hireling rescuers brought an unusually large number of people from the sea and took care of their needs in the newly decorated clubhouse, causing an unusual amount of damage to the carpet and paint. The club had a hastily called meeting, passed a resolution, asking the lifesavers to move to other quarters and in every way separated their activities from that of the club. It seems that in all of this the original agenda had been lost.

The people of God are always in a struggle with the agenda issue. They are like the lighthouse keeper who was given a specified amount of fuel each month with which to light his beacon. His job was to use it judiciously and to make certain there was enough available for an emergency. One day a fisherman, having run out of fuel in his boat, came and asked for a little fuel so he could complete his journey to the shore, and, of course, the lighthouse keeper complied. He was followed by an excursion boat taking tourists to see the deep waters and to appreciate the beautiful shoreline. He found himself in the same predicament, and so to help the people, he gave away some of the precious fuel. Several weeks later a party boat came, filled with revelers. The captain had not made proper provision, so the keeper gave away some more of the precious fuel to help these people also. Finally, on a dark and stormy night, the light was needed, but the keeper had no fuel for the light. Lives were lost unnecessarily. Is this not what happens when the people of God get seduced into personal agendas rather than God's agenda? Energy is used. This seduction obviously happens to churches, but it also occurs to individuals as well. For most modern Christians, the religious life appears to be a good add-on or an acceptable accessory, very much like a better engine or leather upholstery in an automobile. "It should be something to enhance my standing in the community rather than giving me a way to enhance the community," many think. "The programs at church may keep my children off drugs. Who cares about the content of this program? Or the Sunday School lessons and sermons may make me a better businessperson. Who cares about changing my life?" Whatever is being taught is okay as long as it really doesn't go very far.

A young man had become very interested in his faith. He started studying the scriptures and adopting additional ways to deepen his spiritual life and feed his own soul. One day after much struggle, he announced to his pastor that all this religious activity had to cease because his wife was greatly disturbed by it. Her reasoning was very straightforward. She said to her husband, "I like our lifestyle and our place in the community. I'm afraid that if you keep this up, you'll give it all up and become a missionary, or move to the inner city, or join the Salvation Army, or do social work." "It's destroying our marriage," he said, "therefore, I'm changing churches so I can start over, save my marriage, and find a new agenda."

What is God's agenda if it's not to live as a captive of Israel in a nice house, or in our churches, domesticated and well-fed? God began to reveal it to David by reminding him again of his providential care. Notice the "I will's" of God preceded by a series of statements in the first-person singular: "I took you...," "I have been with you...," "I have cut off all your enemies...," "I will make you...," "I will appoint a place for my people..." (vv. 8-10). Here the action shifts from what the king plans to do to a reminder of what God has done. In other words, "I know what I'm doing," God says. "You've done rather well on my agenda so far, and it will be my agenda all the way." This forces us to ask ourselves, "Who is really king here?" If a house for God is to be built, it will be done by God and not by David. Only God can establish the house of Israel and the throne of David forever. Locking up God in a fancy house at this time would not do it.

This passage (2 Samuel 7:1-11, 16) is the foundation for the Messianic hope of Israel. It became the hope for the revival of David's rule after the fall of Jerusalem in 587 B.C.E. It was after this that Israel began to look forward to a new king from the house of David. Here we see that the agenda of God was far greater than the agenda of David.

The Old Testament prophets base their understanding of the kingdom of God on the promise God gave David in 2 Samuel 7. David's agenda was too small; he wanted to establish a rule that would be temporal. He focused on a God located in a nice house, and God would not be localized. Instead, his plan was to establish a kingdom that would begin with David and ultimately change the human heart and extend to all eternity. God will do his agenda. Gabriel's message to Mary speaks of the house of David (Luke 1:32). Peter begins his message at Pentecost in Acts 2:29-30 talking about the house of David. Paul in Romans 1:3 refers to the seed of David.

Now we have waited for his coming. On Christmas we celebrate it, and we must realize that this living, unmanageable God is leading us to something new. Let's be open to his agenda for us. Let's re-examine ourselves and see if perhaps God has an agenda for us greater than anything we can imagine. Let's not force him into our agenda.

Have I Got News For You!

Isaiah 9:2-7

My $favorite$ Christmas story is about the young boy who was given a very important role in the church Christmas play. He was to be the angel and announce the birth of Jesus. For weeks he rehearsed the line that had been given to him, "Behold, I bring you good tidings of great joy." The grandparents got in on it and any time the family was together and the boy was there, they would dress him up in his costume and he would rehearse his part for them, "Behold, I bring you good tidings of great joy." They were certain that when he grew up he would be another Charlton Heston playing Moses because of his dramatic ability. Every time the family gathered, he was given the signal, and on cue he would say, "Behold, I bring you good tidings of great joy."

So the great night came for the Christmas pageant and everybody was in place. All the grandparents and extended family were there. Visitors had come in and all the children were in costumes, complete with bathrobes for the three kings and fake wings and halos for the angels. All the mothers were excited and everyone was really into this thing. As the pageant started, the excitement was electric around the room. The dramatic event in the first part was the announcement by this angel, "Behold, I bring you good tidings of great joy." The light hit this young man and as he stood center stage in the middle of all this excitement, his brain froze. Every grandparent, aunt, uncle, and neighbor came to the edge of their seats, wanting to say it for him. You could see them in unison, mouthing, "Behold, I bring you good tidings of great joy." Still, his brain was frozen; he couldn't say it. He tried it again but it just

41

wouldn't come. So finally in a heroic moment he filled his lungs with breath and blurted out the words, "Have I got news for you!"

I have become convinced that this is exactly what this season is trying to communicate, because the world needs Christmas. I like that frivolous song, "We Need a Little Christmas, and We Need a Little Christmas Right Now." I think the whole universe is trying to say something, and this is the only way the universe knows to say it. Perhaps the church needs to change that line in Scripture from "Behold, I bring you good tidings of great joy," to "Have we got news for you!" For if there is any time we can push back the sorrow of this world, if there is any time that we can unzip the clouds of depression that roll in on our heads, if there is any time we can pierce through the evening news and get a glimpse of hope, it is at Christmastime.

I don't know if the nation is in a recession or depression, but if you listen to the news very much, you are just about ready to give up on life. One story after another of how bad it is fills our family rooms. I felt good the other night before watching the evening news, but when it was over, all I could think of was that I need a little Christmas right now. Don't show me anything else that is bad. However, there are some people who get terribly upset about the $42 billion Christmas machine that rolls through our world. They get upset about it and its excesses. But everything has excesses and America has put excess into Christmas. Push away all the excesses, push away all the tinsel, get rid of all the things that are absolutely un-Christian, come down to the core of it, and what we are trying to do the world needs to hear. We need more than a little Christmas right now; we need a *lot* of Christmas right now.

Celebration is a necessary part of living. The ancient coronation hymn in Isaiah 9:2-7, used originally at the coronation of King Hezekiah, has been picked up by the Christian community as the coronation hymn for the Messiah. This coronation hymn is a theme for trumpets declaring the good news for all humankind, but it has been lost in the shuffle of our celebration and has been muted to the place that it becomes only a tone poem for violins as modern Christians have interpreted it. He comes as light, and he has not abandoned us. People walking in darkness need to understand that.

Sadly enough, the Christian message is no longer played on a trumpet but in many cases on a violin. When Christians try to rescue this message from the secular community, we make it a soothing, gentle lullaby. Religion becomes a spiritual aspirin tablet to be taken with a divine cup of warm milk. Such qualities are symptoms of a sick religion to which this song of Isaiah orchestrated for trumpets brings a tinny response.

This was written to grace the occasion for trumpets, for the anointing of one of Israel's kings, possibly good king Hezekiah. Its measures contain more than mere boastful nationalism. It promises the endurance of the Davidic throne as an instrument of God's service and leading a covenant people called to be his witnesses. Since the first century, Christians have sung it as a coronation song for Jesus. It echoes the hymn in Luke 1:32-33. In our day it vibrates to the music of Handel's *Messiah*. We cannot read it in the flat voice of David's speech. The birth of Christ should be seen as an experience beyond the power of common prose to describe to Christians of every century. For what Christ means to those who have met him and have more than a sentimental acquaintance with him can only be expressed in terms of blaring trumpets. So reading this passage with New Testament eyes we see the following.

He comes as light. The people who wander in darkness have seen a great light. This was sung as background, about King Ahaz and the disastrous alliances and the breakdown of public morality. This reign was also characterized by witchcraft and paganism. It was a reign in which it was said, "Surely, for this word for which they speak there is no dawn" (Isaiah 8:16-22).

This is not unlike our world, which has its own shadow of death — war, poverty, rampant paganism, domestic violence, and the like. "On those who live in deep shadow a light is shown" (v. 2). To that end we follow him.

Light figures brightly in Christ's later disclosure of himself. He announced to Israel at the Feast of Lights in Jerusalem, a celebration that marked the light that followed the night and day during the exodus from Egypt, that he was the light of the world — no wonder they killed him.

On November 11, 1918, the sun rose on the city of Mons, Belgium. All night long, the darkness had been shot through with the lurid flashes of gunfire and the staccato chatter of machine guns that echoed through the deserted streets. But at dawn, the last German outpost withdrew, and from their burned and shattered homes the people streamed into the streets. Down the street came the cry, "Hang out your flags." When the sun rose, it shone on a city of banners and the overwhelming joy of those who, having for four and a half years lived in a land of darkness, now walked free. So it is with Isaiah with his vision. The coronation of Hezekiah provides the opportunity to project the great deliverance onto the screen of the future. The enemy has gone; the captains and kings have departed. Gone is the threat of slavery; gone are the agents of destruction along with their bloody tunics, broken swords, and marching hobnail boots of the oppressor. Now we must proclaim the peace that has fallen over our delivered country. With undying hope, rekindled with every king's coronation in the hope that the ideal king would be sent by God to rule his people, they went on hoping, praying, trusting that he would come — if not now, some other day. That is faith — and when he comes, he will come as light and he will bring peace. It must be remembered that the Hebrew word for peace means not only the cessation of war but a condition of rich, harmonious, and positive well-being. It is living in harmony with ourselves, with others, and with God. This is what Christ brings.

Two artists were commissioned to paint their conception of peace. A panel of distinguished judges would determine which artist had best captured the idea. The winner would get a rich commission. After they had been painting for a long time, the judges assembled to view their works. The first artist unveiled his painting, and there was a beautiful, magnificent pastoral scene, with a farmer coming in after a hard day in the fields. His wife was cooking, his children were playing around the hearth, and all was at peace on this tranquil and beautiful farm. "That's it," said the judges, "but we'll look at the other rendering anyway." They removed the veil of the second painting. Instead of a tranquil, pastoral scene, there was a raging waterfall producing a mist which communicated hostility. But over on the side of the waterfall was a tiny branch of a tree growing out of the rock, and on the end of the branch was a bird's nest. On the edge of the nest was a mother bird, singing her heart out in the midst of the turbulence around her. The judges thought for a moment, then said, "That is peace, tranquility and celebration in the midst of turmoil."

Christ also comes as a royal son (v. 6). "To us a son is given," sang Isaiah. They thought the coronation of the king meant that he would become in some special sense God's son as leader of a messianic people (Psalm 2:7). Christ comes in a far more significant way as God's son, revealing his nature and acting in his power.

God in the flesh was scandalous to the first century mind — too close, too much with us. Christ's ministry and Isaiah's message are what we need. For a nation — the Messiah is God with us — this royal son is God in the flesh: *Wonderful Counselor, Mighty God, Everlasting Father, Prince of Peace* (v. 6). We need him with us. We are lonely and helpless.

Man said to the universe, "Sir, I exist."

However, replied the universe, "The fact has not created within me a sense of obligation."

Christ comes as king forever. Isaiah sang, "There will be no end" concerning the stability of Hezekiah's just order. In a more certain way, we can say that of Christ. William Temple said it truly: "When we serve him in humble loyalty, he reigns; when we serve him self-assertedly, he reigns; when we rebel, he reigns. His reign does not open on our vote. History is a record of his judgments. Happy are they who faithfully obey his rules."

There will be no end.... The rule of Christ has endured wars and rumors of war. His reign has withstood Roman imperialism, Jewish legalism, pagan optimism, medieval institutionalism, excesses of reformers, wars and rumors of wars, youthquake, modern skepticism, southern provincialism, resurgent fundamentalism, and anything else future generations can throw at his reign. It has also been victimized by unprepared preachers, tone-deaf musicians, manipulative members, argumentative deacons, demanding denominations, unloving reformers, and greedy politicians, and still he continues to reign. He provides community in the face of alienation and love and affirmation in a hostile world. His reign is not a porcelain teacup that is easily broken. His reign is an oak tree with deep and abiding roots.

Our world desperately needs to know that not only has God come in Jesus Christ but that he reigns forever and in unexpected ways. Recently, the motion picture *The Bridge Over the River Kwai* was selected as one of the one hundred great films of the twentieth century. It is the story of some British prisoners of war during the Second World War. They were held by the Japanese in northern Burma in very difficult circumstances. It was made into a motion picture and won an Academy Award. Most of us know of it from that standpoint. But Ernest Gordon, theologian and preacher, later to become chaplain at Yale, wrote a book called *Through the River of the Kwai*, which told another side of the story of degradation and desolation experienced by those impoverished prisoners. This book tells how those in the camp interacted with one another. When these young soldiers realized that they were going to be there for a while, they began to have Bible studies and prayed diligently that they could be delivered from their present circumstances. He said, "We knew that the thrust of our praying was to be delivered from this prison camp and that was it. Our praying was shallow and superficial and we were railing against God for letting us be here. But something happened to us and that kind of railing against God disappeared. And we began to move toward a more mature faith. We began to pray about how we could relate to one another in those bad situations. No longer was it 'Why, God?' but it was 'How should we act, God?' " He said the most spiritual moment of his life was Christmas of 1944. Out of deference to the men in the camp, they were not given work detail that day and were given a bit more food. He said that as they moved around in the prison yard, they sensed that things were different. In one of the barracks (basically a thatched hut with dirt floor and open sides where men slept), one soldier began to sing a Christmas carol. It was echoed over in the infirmary where men were dying. Then all around the camp, the men began to sing, and those who could, those who were ambulatory, came to the parade field and sat there in a great circle.

Gordon said, "God touched us that day." He said it was the most sacred event he had ever been involved with. No preaching, nothing of the usual church paraphernalia, just men united by their common misery, singing of God being with them and God's sovereignty, and he said, "We were touched by God." Christmas became real to him when he was touched by God in the surprising place of a Japanese prisoner-of-war camp in northern Burma.

In a world that is as desolate as that camp, we will blow our trumpet. We need to sing the coronation hymn. They need to hear again that God has invaded this earth and he shall reign forever and ever.

Praying With
Bloody Knuckles

Isaiah 61:10—62:3

My wife was conducting a prayer workshop recently and a member of the group told her this true story. She had grown up in London and her pastor walked from his home to the church every day. Along the way he had to pass through some rough sections of town, and as he passed one particular bar there was always the same man loitering outside, very drunk and very loudmouthed. The pastor was really angry at the wasted life and annoyed by the obnoxious taunts of the man. He started praying for the man every time he saw him. This went on for years. Finally, one day this man appeared in the pastor's study and said, "They say you have been praying for me every day and I want to know why you would bother to pray for a man like me." The pastor was able to witness to the man and lead him to Christ! What if he had given up hope and stopped praying?

We have neglected the power of intercessory prayer in our lives and in the lives of others. In our selfish desire to *have* it all and *get* it all we have forgotten to *give* it all. The writer of our text declared in 62:5 that he will not be kept silent but will pester and intercede with God until Jerusalem has experienced a salvation that can be seen as clearly as a bright and burning torch. He is an insistent soul. Like the fifth century ascetic Simeon Stylites, he wants to "batter the gates of heaven with storms of prayer." He is frustrated by God's delay in rebuilding Jerusalem's glory as he had promised. To him, God appears *stuck* concerning his promise, so the prophet constantly reminds him.

Jesus praised importunity and intercession in prayer, but we have neglected both. He prayed for the children (Matthew 19:13), the sick (Mark 7:34), the disciples (Luke 22:31), and his enemies (Luke 23:34). He also prayed for laborers (Luke 10:2) and for all of those who follow him (John 17:20). As Charles Spurgeon reminds us, "Some mercies are not given to us except in answer to importunate prayer. There are blessings which, like ripe fruit, drop into your hand the moment you touch the bough. But there are others which require you to shake the tree again and again, until you make it rock with the vehemence of your exercise, for only then will the fruit fall down." Spurgeon further says, "God will bless Elijah and send rain on Israel, but Elijah must pray for it. If the chosen nation is to prosper, Samuel must plead for it. If the Jews are to be delivered, Daniel must intercede. God will bless Paul, and the nations shall be converted through him, but Paul must pray. Pray he did without ceasing, his epistles show that he expected nothing except by asking for it."

This kind of praying has been called praying with "bloody knuckles." That is, praying with an intensity that opens the door to the needed request and focuses the one praying on the desired result in more than a casual way. In fact, real intercession may achieve its results, but if habitually practiced it has noticeable results in the one who prays. We cannot know the depth of spiritual energy caught in these words. After Job prayed for his friends, the Lord made him prosperous again (Job 42:10). Paul reminds us to pray without ceasing.

The writer's love for Jerusalem and for his God created this intense concern in him. He knew that the happiness and welfare of his family, friends, and larger community depended upon his praying. In fact, intercession is nothing more than love on its knees. When John Knox cried, "God, give me Scotland or I die!" he was praying intensely out of profound love.

The apostle Paul, often misunderstood in our day, interceded for the churches out of a heart of love. "Unceasingly I make intercession for you always in my prayers" (Romans 1:9). This rugged missionary was an intercessor of the highest magnitude. (You may wish to note Romans 10:1, 1 Thessalonians 3:13, Colossians 1:10.)

The finest book on prayer I know is the classic by Harry Emerson Fosdick, *The Meaning of Prayer*. In this work he describes intercession and importunity as dominant desire. He widens the circle of prayer to make it, not the words we utter in public meetings, but rather the total focus of our lives. Our lives always achieve what we pray for when viewed this way, whether the focus is good or evil. As Fosdick says, "Lot wanted Sodom and got it. Judas desired thirty pieces and obtained them. The Bible is full of answered prayers that ruined men." Again and again in history we see the old truth come true: "He gave them their request, but sent leanness into their souls!" (Psalm 106:15).

Also, prayer as dominant desire or "bloody knuckles" praying has greatly influenced the kingdom. Paul, William Carey, and David Livingstone were willing to sacrifice everything to achieve their spiritual ends. This type of praying is not prayer called in to eke out what is lacking in an otherwise contented life, but rather it is life-centering. Bloody knuckles praying is serious business.[1]

In the parables on importunity Jesus focuses on persistence. He wants us, he says, to pray and not lose heart. Our day needs to hear this. We pray in a rather casual way once or twice and give up if nothing happens quickly. It is like turning on a light switch and if the light does not come on we immediately say that we did not believe in electricity anyway.[2]

An out-of-date word that best describes this need is *supplication*. "Supplication means to ask with earnestness, with intensity, with perseverance. It is a declaration that we are deadly serious about this prayer business. We are going to keep at it and not give up."[3] John Calvin writes, "We must repeat the same supplications not twice or three times only, but as often as we have need, a hundred and a thousand times ... we must never be weary in waiting for God's help." As God builds stamina and grit into our spirituality, we today must learn to burn the eternal flame of prayer on the altar of devotion.[4]

This flies in the face of the cardinal virtue of the secular culture — license. Any type of commitment seems to restrict our freedom. We want to go, do, and be whatever the moment makes us desire. This coupled with our aversion to commitment of any kind leads to a certain spiritual atrophy. We want a church to be there for us, but we forget that the church is us! We want others to pay the price spiritually and in other ways so that we can reap the harvest of their labors.

The need of the Christian community today is not larger buildings or smoother organizations. We already reflect the corporate culture around us. Our need is not for slicker programs or more brilliant strategies. We also have vast bureaucracies of specialists at our disposal and still we limp along. Our need is for intercessors who will pray with bloody knuckles for the spirit of the living God to fall on his people. We have enough programs and professionals. We are rich in resources and literature. Our need is for intercessors — *bloody knuckle intercessors.*

It is not a theory but a fact empirically demonstrable that if in any community a large number of people, earnest Christians, unite in unselfish praying for a revival of religious interest, that revival is sure to come.[5]

What are you trying to accomplish that cannot be achieved without a direct intervention from God? "You shall be a crown of beauty ... and a royal diadem. Zion is very precious to the Lord. He awaits to bless his people. They are his glory" (Isaiah 62:3). I am convinced that the Lord loves us and cares more about our concerns than we do. On his timetable he invades our troubles and issues with supernatural power.

In a few days we will start a new year, a new century. We are all carrying into that century the baggage of prior years, the small victories and larger defeats. The scars of past struggles haunt us. This fresh start into a new century gives us an opportunity to pray with bloody knuckles. These past defeats, this residue of scar tissue must be abandoned, and the power that broke through at Bethlehem in the person of Jesus must be called to new challenges in the new century.

There are people and situations that can only be rescued by God's intervention, and we must not give up on praying for them. "When a mother prays for her wayward son, no words can make clear the vivid reality of her supplications. Her love pours itself out in insistent demand that her boy must not be lost. She is sure of his value, with which no outward thing is worthy to be compared, and of his possibilities, which no sin of his can ever make her doubt. She will not give him up. She follows him through his abandonment down to the gates of death; and if she loses him through death into the mystery beyond, she still prays on in secret, with intercessions which she may not dare to utter, that wherever in the moral universe he may be, God will reclaim him. As one considers such an experience of vicarious praying, he sees that it is not merely resignation to the will of God; it is urgent assertion of a great desire. She does not really think that she is persuading God to be good to her son, for the courage in her prayer is due to her certain faith that God also must wish that boy to be recovered from his sin. She rather is taking on her heart the same burden that God has on his; she is joining her demand with the divine desire. In this system of personal life which makes up the moral universe, she is taking her place alongside God in an urgent, creative outpouring of sacrificial love."[6]

Exodus 28:29 gives us an insight into continual intercession and our need for it as practiced by Israel. Every part of the elaborately prescribed dress of the high priest was significant. The breastplate was composed of folded cloth in which there were lodged twelve precious stones in four rows of three, each stone containing the name of one of the tribes. When the priest entered the Holy of Holies he bore on his body the twelve tribes. His very presence at the place of worship was an intercession for the people. He bore on himself, carried in his heart, his profound love and constant intercession for the people. This was a responsibility for the High Priest and a blessing for the people. These people were on his heart. None were excluded from Dan to Beersheba, from the Jordan to the Mediterranean.

So it is with us. Our circle of acquaintances should be carried in our heart — always before the Lord in our prayers. We must lay hold on God with bloody knuckles to be carried along with him in his desires for all humankind.

———————————

1. Harry Emerson Fosdick, *The Meaning of Prayer* (New York: Associated Press, 1915), p. 190.

2. Richard J. Foster, *Prayer: Finding the Heart's True Home* (San Francisco: Harper, 1992), p. 197.

3. Foster, p. 197.

4. Foster, p. 197.

5. Fosdick, p. 190.

6. Fosdick, p. 191.

When God Steps
Out Of Shadows

Jeremiah 31:7-14

Our daughter-in-law designs stage sets for the German theatre. I had always taken this sort of thing for granted until she came into our family. Through Birgit, I was exposed to the subtleties of mood and nuance, of color and properties, of fabric and dimension, and how it all blends with the writer and director to bring the audience to a special point.

After seeing one production of a deeply moving play, the writer and director came from the wings to interact with the audience. Their purpose was to disclose to us what they had in mind, how they went about achieving it, and to reveal the behind-the-scenes thinking of director, writer, and set designer. What was hidden was revealed. What was implicit became explicit.

That is not unlike God in this portion of Jeremiah's word to the captives. Where his purposes had been implicit, he now made them explicit. Heretofore, he had been subtle but now he became vivid. The exile was over. The captives could have their lives and land back. The period of discipline had won them this freedom. God assures them of his purposes and his promises of how he would care for them in the future. He has not abandoned them — rather he demonstrates his deep care for them.

God steps from the shadows, from behind the curtains, from backstage, to show clearly his heart and will for his people. The "I wills" in this passage are a universal message to his church today.

To a large extent God has been in the shadows for us during Advent. At Christmastime, we saw the pageant of the incarnation in all its glory. Now he tells us of the future and our place in it.

Advent and Christmas are not complete unless we see the script for the future. Israel's story is an assurance that God's loving care will triumph.

There would be trials yet to be endured, but through it all the message of Jeremiah remained the same: trust God and move forward.

I. He begins by assuring them that they shall be rebuilt and reunited as a people (vv. 4, 8). "I will ... gather them from the ends of the earth ... a great throng will return."

Israel knew full well that they could not exist fragmented. They needed each other. They could not live independent and alone.

This passage in the lectionary is linked with the New Testament accounting of the "flight into Egypt." That abrupt message was delivered to Joseph in a dream that warned of Herod's brutality and gave the Holy Family a way of escape. The Holy Family further separate themselves from their roots — homeland and security — in order to protect the child. How could they exist alone and vulnerable against the powers of evil either in Israel or Egypt? Would they ever be brought back to the land of their birth, the comfort of their family and faith, the place of support and security? No people on earth knew the value of community more than Israel, and nothing could be more frightening for a young mother and child and their carpenter husband/father than this additional separation. Yet this fulfilled the prophecy about the Messiah coming from Egypt, and also it replicated the trust of Israel (Hosea 11:1) in addition to saving the child's life.

God knows how desperately we need community. "For none of us lives to himself alone and none of us dies to himself alone" (Romans 14:7). He knows we are not complete unto ourselves. We need each other. One man is no man. The community of God's people, first Israel and then the church, is as essential for life as manna in the wilderness — or water in the desert.

The apostle Paul says we are not complete unto ourselves. We are only individual parts of the body. We are of no use unless we are connected. However, in American culture we are still greatly influenced by models such as the Lone Ranger, the Marlboro Man, the rugged individualist, and Frank Sinatra singing what he calls his national anthem, "I Did it My Way."

For those who follow the God of Israel, he promises to give community. He will provide community for us. His church is his gift to us. The church, local and institutionalized, may be out of favor for some parts of the Christian community — but it is still God's gift to us. And, frankly, I think it is the best thing God has going for himself in the world.

Jeremiah talks of the people of God coming from all directions and from all classes to reunite in Jerusalem. They would not trickle in but would come "streaming to the goodness of the Lord" (v. 12). They would not come silently but with a great noise of singing. They would come home, not with mourning and slumped shoulders but with great rejoicing. They would be all kinds of people, blind and lame, as well as strong (v. 8).

This sounds like an early word that Jesus later echoed, "I will build my church" (Matthew 16:18). God will gather; Jesus will build his church. Then why do we fret about his church, his people? He is ultimately in control.

This is also a foretaste of Pentecost. The people had come from the entire known world. They heard a word from God and all heaven broke loose. It happened with strength and power. They came streaming to the goodness of the Lord.

We cannot face the power of the Herods or the loneliness of Egypt alone. We face this and other challenges with the strength of his community around us. That is his promise to us.

II. Also, he promises his leadership. "I will lead them" (v. 9).

His people are only a crowd without his leadership. With his leadership, they become a people, a congregation, and he does this because he relates to them as a father, not as sovereign or tyrant — as a loving father.

We do not value leadership highly in our culture. We mistrust it, try to control it, and seek to subvert it. At best we are ambivalent to it. God chooses to provide his leadership to his church through those he has called to be his leaders in each congregation. Paul notes this in Ephesians 4. He provides leadership for every church, and each leader has the leadership gifts appropriate to the need of the group.

John Clendenan, retired CEO of BellSouth, relates a story from the Galapagos Islands. As you may know, the Galapagos Islands are a uniquely preserved ecosystem, and tourists who visit there are strictly monitored and controlled. They walk on a boardwalk in order not to disturb the soil. They are allowed only to observe the animals and are prevented from ever interacting with them or interfering with their natural behavior. Their assigned guide is trained in eco-management and enforces the rules on the tourists.

One group was observing a nest of sea turtles on the beach from their assigned place. Suddenly, one newly hatched turtle came from the safety of the nest, looked around, and then made his way to the ocean. The distance he had to cover was about thirty yards. Suddenly the sky was filled with sea gulls, their natural enemy, descending on the lone baby turtle. One gull grabbed the turtle in his beak and the others tried to get it from him, causing a large commotion.

The helpless tourists were aghast. "We need to help the innocent turtle," they cried. Hearing this, the guide said the rules would not permit them to go to the rescue — nature had to take its course. The tourists continued to demand that the guide "do something." This was so disturbing that the guide, in order to placate them, relented and went onto the beach and rescued the helpless and half-dead baby turtle. He placed the turtle in the surf. The birds went back to the trees and calm returned. About five minutes later, all the babies in the nest crawled out onto the beach, heading for the surf, and the sky was filled with sea gulls, ready for their evening meal.

The guide and tourists watched helplessly as the entire nest was devoured by the hungry gulls. Then the guide, embarrassed and angry, explained what had happened. One baby sea turtle always goes over the side of the nest to the sea. If he makes it, they know the beach is safe and follow after him; if he doesn't, they know to stay in the nest a little longer. The action of the guide had given a false signal to the baby turtles, and the guide, prompted by the tourists, had been responsible for the loss of the entire nest of babies.

We need leadership and God knows it. Someone must make the difficult and unpopular decisions for the sake of community. Someone must "speak to the people that they may go forward." Someone must deliver the law, and destroy the golden calf. Someone must lead the way. The people need a shepherd, and God will provide one. By giving leadership, God will turn their mourning into joy. The people of God will rejoice and no longer mourn, because leadership is a sign of God's presence in their midst.

He will lead his people on a straight path by rivers of water. This sounds like the twenty-third Psalm. He takes care of his people.

As we view the prospects of the coming new year, we must be certain that his leadership is trusted and followed. It may be difficult or it may be easy, but it will be in our best interest. He will also sustain us beside the river of waters. What more could we ask?

III. He will satisfy the souls of the priests.

These are strange words coming from the pen of Jeremiah in the light of his earlier word about the priests and his struggle with them.

He is actually saying that the sacrifice of the people will be abundant. So abundant that the priests will have enough to eat and not need to exploit the people. Their leadership will be restored to the place of integrity.

Thereby, he will also satisfy the souls of the people. Their long exile, their long journey, their flirtations with false gods while in exile, and the silence of God compounded by the mixed messages from their leaders had damaged their souls. The inner being he will restore.... "He restoreth my soul...."

When God does anything in this world, he does it through his church — but his church at the end of the twentieth century is scarred. The leadership is weak and, in many respects, its soul is unsatisfied. This condition will be remedied. His people will be strengthened and re-seeded for whatever may come in the future.

The Holy Family returned from Egypt to face their Herods. Their strength was a resolute faith in the purpose and providence

59

of God. The opposition of Herod and the slaughter of the infants made it vividly clear to them that the coming of the light provokes the rage of the world.

God has stepped from the shadows to encourage them (and us) that in every circumstance when evil is enraged, God moves to protect his community and the individuals.

The Chinese have a proverb, "Victory has a thousand fathers but failure is an orphan." With the fall of the Berlin Wall and the subsequent demise of Communism, everyone was taking credit. Politicians, educators, and churchmen were working hard to give their version of the story and their part in the victory. There was an account that came after the fall that we must consider. Although free assembly was not permitted by the Communist government, churches could meet if their activities were confined to worship and teaching of the Bible, and they did just that. In fact, Bible study became popular and was well attended. Week after week as the Bible was taught, the desire for freedom — which is so clearly contained in the Bible — began to infect the people. In fact, it flourished in their impoverished souls and pushed them into the streets to pull the Wall down. The fall of Communism was the direct result of the message of God fed to the spiritually hungry population of East Germany.

Herod may win a short-term battle but the family of God will win the ultimate victory.

God has come center stage to speak. We should listen.

In The
Beginning God

Genesis 1:1-5

I like the story of the Middle Eastern prince who fell in love with a beautiful peasant girl. Eventually he proposed marriage and she accepted. Such an event should be marked by a gift of rare beauty, so he searched the empire for the most beautiful diamond to give to her. Obviously, the most beautiful diamond demanded a specific box of rare beauty for the presentation of the precious gem. For this he commissioned the royal cabinetmakers to make the most beautiful box in the kingdom for the diamond.

On the day the diamond was to be presented, appropriate servants, horsemen, and soldiers were summoned to march in the entourage to the peasant girl's cottage. The neighbors and family gathered as they approached. When the prince presented the kingdom's most beautiful diamond, nestled in the kingdom's most beautiful box, they were amazed and awed at the spectacle. The peasant girl studied the gift at length, and then startled the crowd by discarding the diamond and keeping the beautiful box.

This is not unlike what we have done with the miraculous story of the creation given to us in our text. We have spent our days debating the scientific inadequacies of the story or trying to reconcile it to the results of our latest findings in the laboratories. We have completely missed the beauty of the gift that God has given us in this great story.

There is an unforgettable scene in *The King and I*. Anna, the teacher for the king's children, was summoned late one night to the king's audience hall. There she found the Siamese monarch engrossed in reading a large book. "Why, your majesty," she exclaimed, "you're reading the Bible!" The king's response was that Moses was surely an ill-informed man if he thought the world was created in six days. Anna's reply was informed and accurate. "Your majesty, Moses was not a man of science; he was a man of faith."

The account in the Bible is a faith story, not seeking to tell how the world was created scientifically, but by whom and why he created the world. This passage is a gift to us as beautiful as any diamond we have ever seen. Let's hold it up and examine the different facets of it as a jeweler would examine a beautiful stone, hoping to unlock its incomparable beauty.

The original text employs a term for the word *create* which is never used to denote any human activity. It is reserved only for the prerogative of God. The biblical writer is clearly attempting to express something specific. He is saying that what God is creating and making here possesses a quality fundamentally different from anything created and made by human artists or architects. The human artist must wrest the image from the material, which itself sets limits to the freedom that the artist has with it.

Near Clarkesville, Georgia, on the banks of a river there is an old mill and the workshop and gallery of a very gifted potter. He takes the raw clay and creates beautiful pottery that commands very high prices. Each piece has inscribed on it "the Mark of the Potter," which is the name of the shop. That is not what our text for today is saying. That would set limits upon the purposes of God. On the contrary, God created from *nothing* an undistorted reflection of his thoughts, and this creation bears only the mark of God. So God's creation proceeds with a sovereign freedom that has no other influence or limitation.

Some creation myths do not have God doing this kind of creation. They have the gods creating the world out of pre-existing matter. That pre-existing matter sets limits on what the creation can be. That is not so with our God — he created the world out of nothing. In fact, the entire first chapter of Genesis pulsates with the creative nature of God: "God said," "God saw," "God created," "God called," "God made," "God appointed," "God divided," "God ended," "God rested," "God blessed and sanctified."

These words describing the creative activity of God overwhelm us with implications for our lives. It means that I am in the story of creation. My life is fashioned and guided by the same God who put the stars and the sun in place at the beginning of the world. Long before I can think of God and love him, he has already thought of me. Before the foundations of the world, there began the history of a great love and a great search.

God made the world from nothing. I am in it, and therefore I have to accept responsibility for the gifts and talents he has entrusted to me. One day he will inquire, "What have you done with yourself?" We will have to give ourselves back to God just as surely as we have to repay the money we have borrowed from the bank or property we have borrowed from our neighbor. We will be judged by what we have done with what he has given us. He will ask, "What have you done with your body, your gifts, your calling, your family, your wife and children, your friends, and the church I gave you along the way?" There are no excuses. The creative process takes away all the excuses and limits that we have set on ourselves. We cannot blame our lack of stewardship on anything; we must accept it ourselves.

God who confronts us with our stewardship is the father of Jesus Christ. God is faithful and never lets us down. God himself is not a mere part of the world; he is the Lord, the creator of the world, and he dwells in majestical remoteness for all things made, from all creatures. But even though he is the Lord of the world who stretches his commanding hand above the universe, he knows me, and he clasps me to his heart. He will never give me up. I shall always be his child, even when I depart from him or when death comes or the world ends. His faithfulness will never cease.

Luther said, "God created the world out of nothing. As long as you are not yet nothing, God cannot make something out of you." He will never give us up.

"As Jesus was coming up out of the water, he saw heaven being torn open and the Spirit descending on him like a dove. And a voice came from heaven: "You are my son, whom I love; with you I am well pleased" (Mark 1:10-11).

This Sunday we are reminded of the baptism of Jesus. Granted, that theme is secondary in the creation story, yet it is appropriate that at the beginning of the year we recognize its implications in our lives. It is a way of renewing our vows at this Epiphany season. Too often baptism is a rite for small children and is a good excuse for families to get together. The trivialization of this profound moment robs us of its mark, God's mark, upon our lives. This mark has made all the difference.

Baptism is a moment of decision. In the creation story God decided to create order out of chaos. In the baptismal experience we acknowledge our decision to let Christ bring order to our lives which are heretofore chaotic. In fact, chaos describes the condition of at least seventy percent of the adult population. They are "without form and void," totally incapable of loving others. This relationship with fellow humans is manipulative and self-serving. They don't care for anyone else, are unprincipled and governed by their own will. Their total being lacks integrity.

When people at this stage get in touch with their own being it is very painful. They either ride it out unchanged, kill themselves, or decide to change, to convert.

Such conversions can be sudden and dramatic and are God-given. It is as if the person has said, "Anything is preferable to this chaos. I am willing to do anything to liberate myself from this chaos." Nevertheless, a conscious decision has been made for God. As the spirit moved upon the waters at creation, so the spirit moves upon the chaos of human life and brings order. The baptized life is the opposite of the undecided life. Regardless of its form, or the candidate's age, it is the yielded life that began when we were "drowned" in baptismal waters and rose resurrected in the Spirit.

Because of this decision, aimlessness is no longer an option. The decision for Christ has become the first thing in the new life of order and grace. Everything else is secondary. We have but one purpose and that is to express Christ in this world.

This decision for Christ and the subsequent baptism is, in effect, an ordination for us. It is at this point that we are certified for service by the Christian community. Too many in the Christian community fail to see baptism as the certification for ministry. In a real sense all Christians are called, not just the ordained clergy. Baptism puts life in proper perspective. We have but one purpose: to express Christ in the world.

"In the beginning God" ... "and God said that it was good" (v. 9). He begins a work and confirms that it is a good work. As Mark says it, "You are my Son, the beloved, with you I am well pleased." These words of affirmation are words of grace. Grace is what we hunger for. Baptismal affirmation empowers us for ministry. The descent of the dove empowers the baptized not only to defeat every form of evil, but also to be the people of God — as God has called them to be.

Henry David Thoreau once went to jail rather than pay his poll tax to a government which supported slavery. His friend, Ralph Waldo Emerson, visited him in jail. Walking up to the cell Emerson asked with surprise, "Henry, what are you doing in there?" Thoreau never missed a beat as he replied, "Nay, Ralph, the question is what are you doing out there?"[1]

---

1. *Synthesis*, January 12, 1997.

The Man With Two Umbrellas

1 Samuel 3:1-10 (11-20)

The late Dr. J. Wallace Hamilton, who for many years preached at the Pasadena Community Church in St. Petersburg, Florida, tells a wonderful story about the man with two umbrellas. He said that when he crossed the Atlantic one summer he noticed a dark-skinned man sitting in a deck chair, reading the Bible. One day he sat beside him and said, "Forgive my curiosity, but I am a minister. I see you come here every day and read your Bible. I assume you are a Christian, and I am interested to know how it happened."

"Yes," replied the man, setting aside his Bible. "I'm very glad to talk about it. You see, I am a Filipino. I was born in a good home in the Philippines, and some years ago I came to the United States to one of your fine universities to study law. My first night on campus, a student came to see me. He said, 'I have come over to welcome you to the campus and to say to you that if there is anything I can do to help make your stay here more pleasant, I hope you will call on me.' Then he asked me where I went to church, and I named a church that was prevalent in the Philippine Islands but I wasn't very committed to it. He said, 'I can tell you where that church is. It is not easy to find; it's quite a distance away. Let me make you a map.' So he made an outline of the way to the church and he left.

"When I awakened Sunday morning, it was raining. I thought to myself, 'I'll just not go to church this morning. Surely, I can be forgiven for this. It's my first Sunday on a new campus; it's raining hard, and the church is hard to find. I'll get some more sleep.'

67

Then there was a knock on the door. When I opened it, there stood that student. His raincoat was dripping wet, and on one arm he had two umbrellas. He said, 'I thought you might have a hard time finding your church, especially in the rain. I shall walk along with you and show you where it is.' As I got dressed to go, I thought, 'What kind of fellow is this?' As we walked along in the rain under the two umbrellas, I said to myself, 'If this fellow is so concerned about my religion, I ought to know something about his.' I asked, 'Where do you go to church?' 'Oh,' he replied, 'My church is just around the corner.' I said, 'Suppose we go to your church today, and we'll go to my church next Sunday.' I went to his church and I've never been back to my own. After four years, I felt it was not the law for me but rather I felt a call of God to the ministry. I went to Drew Seminary, was ordained a Methodist minister, and received an appointment to a Methodist church in the Philippines. I am a bishop now of the Methodist church in the Philippines."

The most important man in this story is not the Methodist bishop but the man with the two umbrellas. Now to the biblical story before us. What made the young Samuel so open to the call of God that strange night in Eli's house? "Speak, your servant is listening" (v. 9). The young boy answered quickly and easily after he had figured out who was calling to him. But he did not arrive at the conclusion as easily as we make it sound in sermons and Sunday school lessons. Samuel had been under the wing of Eli, the priest of Shiloh and a judge of Israel, ever since he had been weaned. Eli was overseeing his service as a lifelong Nazarite. Eli had no joy in his own two sons, Hophni (tadpole) and Phinehas (the Nubian), for they were reprobates and had no regard for God, even though they were priests of the Lord. Naturally, this made Samuel more an apprentice or, even more, a surrogate son (v. 16). It pleased Hannah, Samuel's mother, for this was the child she had prayed for and had promised to God.

During the nights, Samuel heard a voice calling to him, and he awakened the old priest. "Here am I. You called me?" "You are mistaken. Go back to bed," the old man said. This occurred the second, and then the third time. Finally, as Eli was dozing off and the wise old priest was thinking that perhaps this was not an event that could be ignored, his spiritual senses kicked in and he knew something unique was transpiring here. "Go back to bed and hear the divine revelation." The source of the interruption was none other than the God of Israel. Samuel would not have been able to respond to the call of God had it not been for the influence of old Eli.

The influence of one life upon another is powerful. We are all tremendously affected by what other people do or say. There is an invisible pull of one life upon another. For example, in a Nazi concentration camp where Martin Niemoller was imprisoned, a Nazi agent was placed in a cell next to that of Dr. Niemoller in the hope of converting the Christian minister to totalitarianism. After some days of observing God's prisoner (as he was called), his habit of devotion, his unfettered faith in the ultimate triumph of righteousness, the Nazi officer called for a copy of the Bible, whereupon he was promptly removed from the jail.

Once, in the Bureau of Standards in Washington, D.C., a tiny tube containing less than 1/2,000 of an ounce of radium was accidentally dropped and broken on the hardwood floor. With a camel's hair brush, they swept up the radium. Then they washed the floor to get the rest of it. But enough remained to render four more washings necessary. Each yielded more radium. Finally, a carpenter scraped the floor three years later, the shavings were burned, and the ashes were found to be strong in radium.

We cannot get rid of influence. The Bible tells us that no man lives or dies to himself (Romans 14:7). To influence is to sway, to affect, to be acted upon by mental, moral, or spiritual power. The Bible illustrates influence as a leaven (Matthew 13:33), as sound spreading forth (1 Thessalonians 1:8), or as salt (Matthew 5:17), cancer (2 Timothy 2:17), ointment or fragrance (Proverbs 27:18).

Influence is not an option for us; we all have it. The option is the kind of influence or how we will exert our influence. Everyone is contagious. Hannah, the mother of Samuel, knew this. She wanted old Eli to influence her boy. He was mature in the faith. He was someone with whom Samuel could be close. This kind of closeness makes one God's usher, leading souls God's way by a relationship of trust, friendship, mutual support, and loving honesty. I strongly believe the living Christ is present in this influence. Christ gets between the two people in the influence, the witness and the listener. Christ himself finally meets the other person, using the witness only as an usher. This is a sacred witness because Jesus is present. He lives and this is the reason the miracle happens — the miracle in which we, the talker and the listener, are both converts. I must look again at Christ because the other points to him as well. It is an experience that can only be called a "miracle of betweenness," a factor in the Christian faith. This kind of influence, or the miracle of betweenness, enabled Samuel to hear the call of God for his life. Whether or not Samuel would have found his way without Eli is a matter of speculation. The fact is he did have the influence of Eli which held him so that he could hear the call of God.

The call of God is indispensable for the Christian leader. It is a time for us to understand that we are discussing the most sacred part of a minister's life, the holy of holies, the place where he loses control of the direction of his life and Someone else takes over. Paul Scherer has said, "We should ... clear out of the road all the nonsense we have picked up, if any, in the matter of the call of the Christian ministry. There is such a call and when it comes, it comes straight from God. I believe with all my heart a man must hear it and feel its imperious constraint before he can ever give himself with any wholehearted devotion and abiding wonder to this stewardship of the gospel."[1]

The apostle Paul in Ephesians 4:11 regarded the office of pastor as a definite appointment of the Holy Spirit. He was also certain that a divine call by Christ had placed him in the ministry (1 Timothy 1:12). A pastor who sees his ministry only as a vocational choice soon learns the folly of his choice. Any man who selects the ministry as a profession will be studying insurance after the first meeting of his official board. The call of the eternal must ring through the rooms of his soul as clearly as the sound of the morning bell rings through the valleys of Korea calling the people to prayer and praise. Ralph Waldo Emerson has said that men whose duties are done beneath the lofty and stately domes acquire a dignified stride and a certain stateliness of demeanor, and I believe that is also true of preachers of the gospel. Understanding that one is called and an acknowledgement of that call give a compass that guides the Christian leader in his intellectual journey. It is an aimless life that does not have this compass.

The Bible is filled with accounts of God calling people in a special way and to a peculiar service. Those who are called of God stand in the best biblical tradition. God called Moses (Exodus 3:10). God called Isaiah (6:9). He called forth Jeremiah (1:5). Saul of Tarsus was dramatically converted and became a chosen vessel in Acts 9:15. To the eleven Jesus said, "You did not choose me, but I chose you and appointed you to go and bear fruit — fruit that will last ..." (John 15:16). The scriptures make crystal clear the fact of the divine call given by God to specific people for specific purposes is beyond debate. The mistake we make is to demand that God speak the same way to each of us. There is only one "road to Damascus" experience in the New Testament, but there are many conversions and many are called. Paul's experience on that road is not a model for all conversions and calls. That he was converted and called is all that matters.

In the Bible we see Amos, a poor herdsman from Tekoa. As his campfire burned, he heard the call and saw the beckoning hand. "The Lord took me from tending the flock and said, 'Go, prophesy to my people Israel' " (Amos 7:15). He spoke with passion against the years of dark doings in high places, wealth breeding laziness, rampant injustice.

But Isaiah was a friend of kings, cultured and courtly. "In the year King Uzziah died I saw the Lord." Mourning the fall of the king, he heard the voice of God. His answer was, "Here am I. Send me."

Jeremiah, brooding about vocational direction, heard the voice of God saying to him, "Before thou camest forth out of the womb I sanctified thee and I ordained thee a prophet" (Jeremiah 1:5). It was a clear call, greatly feared and reluctantly accepted. The biblical evidence has no set pattern, but a strong sense of "the hand of the Lord was upon me" is apparent. The manner of one's call may be different, but there is always a sense of divine initiative.

Now we come to the real issue, which is whether we are one-umbrella Christians or two-umbrella Christians. A one-umbrella Christian denies his call and influence. But a two-umbrella Christian answers God's voice and understands his call and the power of influence and focuses it properly. Anyone can be a one-umbrella Christian. A one-umbrella Christian is a consumer of religion; he just picks and chooses and consumes it. But a two-umbrella Christian is a disciple of Jesus Christ. A one-umbrella Christian says, "My needs first." A two-umbrella Christian says, "The kingdom of God first." A one-umbrella Christian says, "What meets my convenience comes first." But the two-umbrella Christian says, "What reaches people for Jesus Christ must come first." A one-umbrella Christian says, "My group, me first." The two-umbrella Christian says, "The kingdom first," and he makes his decisions based upon the kingdom, not on his own selfishness. We need to be two-umbrella Christians. A one-umbrella Christian says, "How little can I give and get by?" A two-umbrella Christian says, "How much can I give when I realize what he gave?" A one-umbrella Christian samples sermons and lessons, becomes a gourmet of religion, but a two-umbrella Christian follows Jesus. Wherever he leads I'll go, whatever commitment it takes — that is what the two-umbrella Christian does.

This has only been a way of describing discipleship in the light of our call and influence. We must pick up the second umbrella. We need to move from comfort to discipline. We need to move from consumerism to dedication. We should remember that Jesus said, "Take up your cross and follow me." Two-umbrella Christians change their world, thus fulfilling their call.

---

1. Paul Scherer, *For We Have this Treasure* (New York: Harper Brothers, 1944), pp. 4-5.

Defining
Moments

Jonah 3:1-5, 10

Throughout the Bible God caused defining moments
in order to prepare leadership to begin new chapters in salvation
history. When any person is confronted with this sort of event, it is
usually the time when one's deepest values come in conflict with
life situations. These circumstances give each of us the opportunity to choose a path. Over the years the cumulative effect of these
decisions form character. There is no doubt that we are each the
sum total of our personal decisions.

> *To every man there openeth*
> *a way and ways and a way.*
> *The high soul treads the highway,*
> *the low soul gropes the low,*
> *and in between on the misty flat*
> *the rest drift to and fro.*[1]

There are choices that challenge us in a deeper way by asking
us to choose between two or more ideals in which we deeply believe. Character is formed in these situations because we commit
ourselves to irreversible courses of action that shape us personally
and professionally. These defining moments uncover things in us
that have been hidden, and we discover things about ourselves and
reveal them to others. It is in these times that we discover whether
we will live up to our personal ideals or only pay lip service to
them. Here we discover something in a very painful way — we
discover who we really are.

73

This has happened to all of God's leaders. For example, Abraham had his defining moment when he heard the voice of God calling him from the security of Ur to the insecurity of the life of a nomad. Can you imagine the conversations that took place in that home and the explanations to the extended family? Abraham obviously spoke very forcefully and convincingly to those who would make this trek with him. Through his decision God began his work of salvation.

We see how Joseph, best-loved son of his father but hated by his older brothers, was sold into slavery. He was brought into Potiphar's household as a servant and soon proved so trustworthy that he was put in charge of his entire house. Only a short time passed until Potiphar's wife repeatedly tempted Joseph to have an affair with her. This was his defining moment. When he refused her, she falsely accused Joseph and he was sent to prison. His decision planted the seeds that produced the exodus.

What about Moses, who faced his defining moment before the burning bush? He very reluctantly gave up the security and obscurity of a shepherd's life to face Pharaoh, and to herd a bunch of grumbling slaves to freedom with Pharaoh's armies in hot pursuit. The defining moment of Moses led to the birth of a new nation.

Of course, Jesus is the ultimate example of facing life's defining moments. After his baptism, he was taken into the wilderness and for forty days and nights struggled with his mission. The author of his defining moment was the devil himself. Only after Jesus faced Satan and made his choice clear did the devil leave him. This was the defining moment that began the ministry of Jesus and changed the world forever.

Jesus had a way of producing defining moments for the disciples as he called each of them to follow him. The first ones to face this were Simon and his brother Andrew, whom Jesus called as they were fishing along the shore of the Sea of Galilee. Farther along the lake Jesus found the sons of Zebedee, James and John, mending nets in their boat. He called them and they immediately left their boat and their father and followed him. The defining moments and the responses of these disciples, as well as the others, have had an impact on history that continues to this day.

Modern history has taken turns that seem improbable due to the response of individuals to their defining moments. We will never forget the day or the event when Rosa Parks, an African-American domestic worker, refused to surrender her seat on a bus to a white man. This event occurred on December 1, 1955, in Montgomery, Alabama. Mrs. Parks, prior to her arrest on this occasion, had observed the quiet strength of her mother and grandmother. She had tried unsuccessfully to register to vote and had experienced public humiliation when bus drivers insisted that blacks pay at the front, then enter by the back door to sit in the back of the bus. In fact, sometimes the drivers would take the fare, then shut the door and drive off, leaving Rosa or other blacks standing there. This continuing mistreatment, not only of herself, but also of the black race in countless ways, culminated in producing the defining moment for Rosa Parks. After this incident, a 382-day bus boycott eventually led to the desegregation of the city's buses. Rosa Parks is known as "the Mother of the Civil Rights Movement," but she has said that she would like for people to know that her faith in God, her religious convictions, and her church helped give her the strength to meet her defining moments with courage, which in turn ignited the national civil rights movement and changed the social fabric of America.

My good friend, Senator Max Cleland, has faced and continues to face more defining moments than any of us can ever imagine. Max says in his book, *Strong at the Broken Places*, that as a child and adolescent he was intent on testing his limits, so it was natural for him to become a second lieutenant in the U.S. Army through ROTC. After college and graduate school, he volunteered for Vietnam in 1967. While there on active duty, an exploding grenade cost him both legs and his right arm. His first defining moment came on the battlefield before being evacuated — he decided that he wanted to live. Max's story not only involves extreme physical and mental anguish, but turns on the fact that he made a key inner discovery. As he has often said, "After all human effort is spent, another source of strength is available." Max continues to face defining moments that, in his words, "help me become strong at the broken places." Through his public service, both volunteer and elected, Max has made a difference in the quality of life for Georgians, and now, as a United States senator, all Americans.

Now we come to look at our scripture for the third Sunday of Epiphany. The story of Jonah shows beyond the shadow of a doubt that God chooses to use reluctant people to do his work. Jonah definitely did not volunteer to go to witness to the people of Nineveh. The story has several unusual twists and turns and the bottom line seems to be that if at first you don't respond correctly to your defining moment, you'll meet it again and again!

Jonah had successfully lived under the radar of public recognition all of his life, and he liked it that way. He was satisfied with a small vision and little responsibility, virtually no pressure. There is safety in smallness of vision and narrowness of mind and heart, and he had found it. Then God interrupted this narrow rut and presented to Jonah a series of defining moments that challenged him to leave his comfort zone. Actually, that is an understatement of how Jonah felt about the whole situation. However, these challenges revealed much about Jonah and about God, as well. All of Jonah's presuppositions concerning life were challenged by his call from God. He was stretched between two value systems. He never expected to have his comfort area and his narrow lifestyle interrupted by God's demand that he catch the vision of a larger world.

Jonah was basically working with rural people and he sincerely believed that God had always been partial to rural people. The entire Hebrew Bible reflects this belief. Life began in a rural setting (the Garden of Eden), and cities were cesspools of evil (Sodom and Gomorrah). Had not all the prophets spoken against the cities and then retreated to the countryside for rest and spiritual reflection? Not only was Nineveh urban, but also it was not even in Israel. It was the greatest of the capitals of the Assyrian Empire located on the left bank of the Tigris River in northeastern Mesopotamia (known today as Iraq). Jonah thought God was a tribal deity, limited to Israel. How could God possibly be concerned about the Assyrians? Why should God or Jonah care about them?

Jonah's God was too small, his vision was too limited, and his heart was too cold and hard to get involved in this operation. So he did the only thing he knew to do — he ran away! He assumed that if he could get out of God's territory, he would escape the claims of God and avoid this defining moment. His method of doing this was to take the next boat to Tarshish, the Timbuktu of the ancient world. You know the story. In his absolute defiance, his determined disobedience to the command of God, Jonah ran to the nearest boat dock (Joppa) and bought a ticket to the farthest place it would sail. The interesting thing is that Jonah was found sleeping through a raging storm that frightened even seasoned sailors. When confronted by the captain, Jonah told them that the Lord was punishing him for his disobedience and for them to throw him overboard, and the storm would subside. However, the heathen sailors had more compassion for Jonah than he had shown for the Ninevites and continued to try to row the boat to safety. Finally, they did throw him overboard, and immediately the sea calmed. They were so fearful of the Lord that they offered a sacrifice to the Lord and made vows. Perhaps this was their defining moment!

So this is how Jonah found himself in the stomach of the great fish for three days and three nights. The Lord dealt with Jonah and finally commanded the fish to throw Jonah up on dry land. We don't know how much time elapsed before the Lord gave Jonah instructions once again to go and preach to the Ninevites. He told Jonah what to say as he preached, and to Jonah's surprise and dismay, the people of Nineveh believed, called a fast, and put on sackcloth, from the greatest to the least of them. The king, when he heard of this, arose from his throne, threw off his robe, put on sackcloth, and sat on the ashes. How could Jonah ever have imagined this turn of events? The king even issued a proclamation that called on all his people to fast, put on sackcloth, and call on God earnestly, that each might turn from his wicked and violent ways. When God saw their deeds, he relented concerning the calamity which he had declared he would bring upon them, and he did not do it. This king took his duties seriously and heard the word of the Lord. He met his defining moment with amazing haste and solidarity. Everyone repented except Jonah. He was disgusted and irate with God for being gracious, compassionate, slow to anger, and abundant in loving kindness. What a pitiful man Jonah turned out to be — whining at God because he blessed his preaching, allowing him to be the vessel that delivered the message of God's displeasure with the people of Nineveh and, therefore, the instrument of their revival and survival. He was so upset that he begged God to let him die. If there had been a comedy network in the day of Jonah, some comedian could have had a wonderful time with this story, pretending to be Jonah. I'll leave it to your imagination to complete that scene.

At first, this seems to be a strange story to have as a lectionary reading for Epiphany. At closer inspection, the spirit of Epiphany shines throughout the story. It has been suggested that this is the John 3:16 passage of the Old Testament. This story makes it clear that God is always eager to save a heathen people and that in the heart of the heathen there is always the possibility of response and repentance to God's message (v. 5). Jonah did not have the spirit of Epiphany but it is clear that God can hit straight with a crooked stick. He accomplishes his purposes even when we fail the defining-moment test.

Now we come to the time when we must decide what this means to us today. It is time to look at our lives and think about how God would grade us on our response to personal defining moments. Remember that King David, with all his wonderful qualities, failed one particular defining moment when he lusted after Bathsheba (and acted upon that lust). There was no turning back after the deed was done. There is no escape from logical consequences.

Do you remember the scene from the movie, *Titanic*, when the captain was confronted and strongly urged by the owners of the vessel on her maiden voyage to accelerate the speed and compromise on safety standards? He failed his defining moment miserably when he succumbed to their badgering and called for "full speed ahead." Other ships in the area began to radio warnings of wandering icebergs, and one ship, the *Californian*, tried twice to radio the *Titanic*, but was cut off because, after all, wealthy Americans had messages they needed to radio to the states. The result is now on the big screen for all the world to view the horror and loss of life. Over 1,500 souls were drowned under the icy waves. A defining moment affecting countless lives of families and friends of the victims was ignored in the midst of pressure from the rich and famous.

What about your personal life? What about your family life, your business life? Defining moments are sometimes as insignificant as signing your name to a half-truth, or skimming just a little off the top of a bank deposit, or calling home to say you were detained at the office when you were really somewhere else. You can provide your own scenario from your daily activities. Like Jonah, we often try to run away from our defining moments, but these times have a way of becoming like the television reruns — we see them over and over, and it is not always a pretty scene.

Churches also have defining moments. There is probably not a pastor alive who has not witnessed or been a part of a church which just completely failed the defining moment test. Individual churches have decisions to make concerning issues that are soul-wrenching. For example, during the time that Rosa Parks faced her defining moment, there were churches in Alabama that also had to face this issue. History shows that any pastor of a downtown church in any city in Alabama who preached racial inclusiveness faced persecution from his congregation and each was systematically replaced over a short period of time. These churches failed the test — they completely ignored the Biblical admonition to love one another; that there is no difference in God's eyes of Jew or Greek, black or white, male or female. Whoever heard of Epiphany in a situation like segregation?

My dear friend, Jimmy Allen, has written a book that will tear at your heart. *The Burden of a Secret* is his sharing of his personal grief and the grief of his family concerning the disease that took the life of his daughter-in-law and baby grandsons. Lydia had been given tainted blood during the delivery of their first child and given this information when the second baby became gravely ill and was diagnosed as having AIDS. Lydia and three-year-old Matt also tested positive. Only the father, Scott, was free of the virus. At the time, Scott was the associate pastor of a church in Colorado, and shortly after telling his parents the shocking news, he also informed his pastor. The pastor asked for Scott's resignation on the spot, and though Scott did not agree, he later found a letter on his desk

79

"accepting" his resignation. The majority of the governing body of the church agreed and simply accepted his resignation. The excuse for this action may be that this was so early in the AIDS epidemic that people were hysterical concerning it. This was the fall of 1985 and not much was known except that it was a deadly and contagious disease.

This church (and I am sure that there have been others) completely and utterly failed its defining moment. The AIDS epidemic, like the segregation issue, has provided the church with unusual opportunities to express loving compassion and to be the Christ figure to victims and their families. Dr. Allen expresses this eloquently in the book: "The church is at its best when it escapes the captivity of its culture, and strips down to the basic task of loving, serving, and sharing the mystery of God's presence with hurting people."[2]

We need to understand, especially at this Epiphany season, that it is the season to proclaim the glad tidings of God to all those who need to hear. People are hurting in so many ways. People are called upon to carry enormous burdens, and they desperately need help. They need to experience the touch of God as expressed through the church and through individuals. We must proclaim the gospel to all people by all means possible. We must be willing to reach out to offer a healing touch not only to people who are dying of a physical illness, but also to those whose souls are in jeopardy. We do not need to be judge and jury, ready to condemn people. What the world needs more than anything is the loving, compassionate, healing touch that can only come through the love of Christ dwelling in each of us. Jimmy Allen says that he and his family, though they found little help in the church, experienced the support of friends, the love of family, and the grace of God.

Imagine that your church is facing one of these defining moments. What do you think the outcome will be? Will your church pass or fail?

Now think about yourself and your own personal defining moments. What will your "report card" reveal? Will you pass or fail? Will you be like the poet, Robert Frost, in the last verse of the poem, "The Road Not Taken," when he says:

I shall be telling this with a sigh
somewhere ages and ages hence:
Two roads diverged in a wood, and I —
I took the one less traveled by,
And that has made all the difference.

And now to each of you, both as individuals and as members of a corporate body, listen to the words of Jesus calling us to our defining moment, saying, "Come, follow me."

---

1. John Oxenham, *William Barclay Study Daily Bible: Mark* (Philadelphia: The Westminster Press, Second Edition, 1956), p. 10.

2. Jimmy Allen, *Burden of a Secret* (Nashville: Moorings, 1995), p. 210.

Famous
Last Words

Deuteronomy 18:15-20

---

*"**Heavier-than-air** flying machines are impossible."*
— Lord Kelvin, President, Royal Society, 1895
  "This 'telephone' has too many shortcomings to be seriously considered as a means of communication. The device is inherently of no value to us." — Western Union internal memo, 1876
  "Louis Pasteur's theory of germs is ridiculous fiction." — Pierre Pachet, Professor of Physiology at Toulouse, 1872
  "Airplanes are interesting toys but of no military value." — Marechal Ferdinand Foch, Professor of Strategy, Ecole Superieure de Guerre
  "Everything that can be invented has been invented." — Charles H. Duell, Commissioner, U.S. Office of Patents, 1899
  "Are you sure the power is off?"
  "The odds of that happening have to be a million to one!"
  The last words of outstanding individuals have fascinated me for some time. Somehow their whole lives are measured by their words at the end of their lives. From their words we can measure our understanding of the world. This fourth Sunday of Epiphany brings us to some famous last words — those of Moses as he was preparing to leave his people. For forty years he had led Israel across the Red Sea and the burning desert. For forty years he had suffered their rebellion, immaturity, ingratitude, and complaining. Now it was time for him to say good-bye. After the long course his task had been completed. The plagues were over, the shadow of the death angel was gone, the sea of chaos crossed, and the murmuring of the people was over. Their thirst had been quenched and

their hunger filled. Now he stood upon his mountain as the people worshiped in exultation in the presence of Jehovah God. Moses knew that he had truly been called of God to do this task, but who would follow after him? What kind of leader would the people select for the future? Of course, he was interested in who would follow him. These were his people. They were a part of his very soul and he would not entrust them to just anyone.

In this part of his famous last words he outlined the type of leader they would need for their future. These are as appropriate for us today as they were for the Israelites at this moment in their history.

Moses knew that leadership was important to the task before them. As we look back from our vantage point, we know that Israel did not have another superlative leader for another two hundred years. This period of their history reflects their need for leadership.

Our need today is for leaders who fit the profile outlined by Moses. The church needs leaders — not power holders, not hype artists, not influence peddlers or manipulative demagogues.

In the eighteenth century, Europe desperately needed spiritual leadership. Revolution was raging in France, and England was in moral decay. God supplied the needed leadership in George Whitfield and John and Charles Wesley, who became flaming evangels, carrying the message of God throughout America and England. John Hudson Taylor founded the China Inland Mission. John Barnaroll began mission work in London which rescued and trained 70,000 homeless children. William Booth organized the Salvation Army, which is now a worldwide organization for righteousness. God uses leaders to save civilization and give it spiritual direction.

We live in a culture that is afraid of leadership. We now believe that a decision is good only if a large number of people have been a part of making it. We are enamored by the thought that anybody's word is as good as anyone else's word. Our credo is to lead from the middle, suffer fools gladly, preach from the back of our heels rather than the balls of our feet, and conceal competence in the interest of extending democracy.

We seem confused about the role of leadership and the need for leadership. Leadership can be defined as the discipline of deliberately exerting special influence within a group to move it toward goals of beneficial permanence that fulfill the group's real need.

Vince Lombardi said that leadership is the ability to get a team to do what they do not want to do so that they can be what they have always wanted to be.

The group is not served when no one is at the wheel. When we enter an airliner, we do not want to see the captain carrying a textbook on flying. I have made many trips overseas, but I have never seen the captain let the passengers vote as to whether he should turn on the radar.

George Buttrick, longtime pastor of the Madison Avenue Presbyterian Church in New York City, was asked if he would have a layman preach on Layman's Sunday, and his reply was classic: "When they have Layman's Day at Mount Sinai Hospital and let me operate." A leader is one who is trained, competent, a visionary, and an agent for change. Regardless of its theology, denomination, or form of worship, no church ever makes progress toward its goals without a strong leader at the top.

I recently attended a denominational meeting which had a "break-out" session for the laymen. Its purpose was to seek ways in which they could become more involved in ministry. No mention was made of "gifts for ministry" or needs in the community. The sole concern seemed to be to find ways to keep their pastors from leading. Yet they complained about the ineffectiveness of their churches.

What passes for church democracy and congregational leveling is unbiblical and unwise. Everybody's business is no one's business and it demonstrates a basic distrust within the body.

The pastor of a neighboring church called me for lunch one day. He sat across the table from me with tears in his eyes as he told me that he had been having difficulty with leading his church, especially in the area of preaching and worship. It seems that he moved the pastoral prayer to another position in the service. This created such an uproar that a special congregational meeting was called and they approved a resolution that instructed him to meet with a group of laypersons regularly concerning the order of worship. He was also instructed to preach only from texts and subjects approved by the committee and told that he must read from a manuscript.

Leadership is God's gift to his church. In Ephesians 4:11-14, he gives gifts to his people as individuals and the gift of leadership to the community of faith.

A church in Florida which had experienced unusual growth with a strong leader and preacher instructed its pastoral search committee to find a pastor that was just the opposite. "We need a visitor, someone who will give us care," they said. "Preaching and leadership is not that important." The new pastor, who had great gifts in pastoral care, was ineffective in areas that had built the church. He was asked to resign in eighteen months because of falling attendance and budget. Leadership built the church and leadership will sustain the church.

A sower went forth to sow — not to build consensus or to be well-liked. A teacher went forth to teach! A leader went forth to lead! A preacher went forth to preach! The line of penetration runs from the pulpit to the pew to the pavement.

Moses knew the need for leadership as well as the power of leadership. His legacy may be the law or the journey to the promised land in the minds of some, but he knew that his legacy was the gift of leadership that produced the Hebrew religion. The people were fragile and could not survive the new situation without leadership, so he outlined his understanding of what was to be required of the next leader.

This new leader should be like Moses at Horeb (Sinai) mediating a fresh normative revelation of God. He should speak with God face to face and reflect the divine glory — a mediator between God and his people. He should come from among the people. A stranger who was not familiar with their situation could not be their leader. The responsibility of the leader was to speak God's word, and the responsibility of the people was to hear and do the word. The test of the leader was whether the forth telling actually worked out in their lives. "The proof was in the pudding."

When these *famous last words* of Moses are closely examined, we see that Jesus fits this profile perfectly, and ultimately he became the head of the church and the leader of the people of God. As Moses led them from bondage in Egypt, so Christ leads from the bondage of sin. Like Moses, his life was spared in infancy. Like Moses, he was a powerful intercessor for his people, speaking with God face to face and reflecting the divine glory. Like Moses, he was a mighty prophet in word and deed who revealed God's will and purpose. Christ was a mediator of the covenant and leader of the people.

Jesus had a job to do and he got it done. He directed the activities of that band of followers. He did not begin the day by asking the disciples each morning, "Where shall we go today?" He was in charge. The modern church leader (pastor) has been too influenced by the miracle of dialogue, group dynamics, clinical pastoral education, and congregational democracy. He/she preaches "from the back of the heels rather than the balls of the feet."

Moses did not ignore the diversity of gifts, but he understood it and was pleading for a leader who would lead. When everyone is responsible for everything, no one is responsible for anything. The leader feeds the community of faith so that the community of faith can feed the world (Ephesians 4:12,13). There is a wisdom in congregations; they follow only as long as they are certain that the under-shepherd has contact with the Great Shepherd. More churches have been hurt by pastoral inaction than by pastor domination.

The leader Moses profiles is to be a mediator between God and his people. His responsibility is to listen to God and then to speak to the people. The people should hear the word and do it. The vision of God for his people is all-important. A group will disintegrate without a vision.

Fortune magazine recently profiled the CEOs of the ten best corporations in America. They wanted to know what they had in common, what their strengths were. What can be learned from them? Each one possessed a vivid vision for what they wanted their organization to do. This vision dominated everything that they did and every decision that they made. They also possessed the ability to communicate that vision to their constituency. They were able to focus the resources of the organization to accomplish the vision.

Martin Luther King, Jr., made a speech in 1963 at the Lincoln Memorial in Washington, D.C. He expressed his vision for America. He wanted "the riches of freedom and the security of justice" for all people. "I have a dream that my four little children will one day live in a nation where they will not be judged by the color of their skin, but by the content of their character. I have a dream ... of that day when all God's children, black men and white men, Jews and Gentiles, Protestants and Catholics, will be able to join hands and sing in the words of the old Negro spiritual, "Free at last! Free at last! Thank God Almighty we are free at last!"[1]

---

1. Stephen B. Oats, *Let the Trumpet Sound: The Life of Martin Luther King, Jr.* (New York: Harper & Row, 1982), p. 260-261.

What It Takes
To Be A Winner

Isaiah 40:21-31

This text for the fifth Sunday of Epiphany is probably the most sublime passage of Scripture in the Old Testament. It is the poetic description of the soaring of eagles. The Jewish people were in exile and it is likely that every one of them had looked up at the sky, seen eagles soaring, and cried out in their souls to the Lord to give them the freedom of the eagles. They were beginning to doubt that God cared for them. They desperately needed assurance that God was still in charge and that he cared about their plight. Isaiah, the great prophet of the exile, was trying to give them encouragement and so, very eloquently he said these words:

> *Do you not know?*
> *Have you not heard?*
> *The Everlasting God, the Lord, the Creator of the ends*
> *   of the earth does not become weary or tired.*
> *His understanding is inscrutable.*
> *He gives strength to the weary.*
> *And to him who lacks might he increases power.*
> *Though youths grow weary and tired,*
> *And vigorous young men stumble badly,*
> *Yet those who wait for the Lord will gain new strength;*
> *They will mount up with wings like eagles,*
> *They will run and not get tired,*
> *They will walk and not become weary.*

Is your mood that of weariness? Goodness knows, we're entitled! This is what the Jewish people felt in their exile. They were ready to give up, and Isaiah was trying to tell them that power and strength were available to them in the renewable form of soul power. Hopeful waiting would put them well along the way to running a successful race. They needed to know the key ingredients to being able to win over their own weariness and discouragement, and that is what Isaiah gave them in this poetic expression of God's gift of courage. Soul power is available to each of us just as it was to God's people in exile, and this is what will win the race of life.

Athletes who participate in the Olympic Games know well the importance of hopeful waiting. It is the time when long hours are spent in practice, skills are honed, timing is perfected. All in all, it is a very busy time — but it is waiting for the moment of performance, of hoping for the victory that the waiting has prepared them for.

The summer of 1996 brought the Olympics and two and a half million visitors to the city of Atlanta. Not only had the participating athletes been in a period of hopeful waiting but so had the city of Atlanta and all the surrounding areas. The city had to be ready to greet and host these millions of people. It was an overwhelming task, but everyone got in the spirit of anticipation, of hopeful waiting.

There have been many stories of Olympic heroism, of athletes who had to overcome incredible odds in order to participate in an historic event. Nadia Comaneci was the first young lady in Olympic competition to ever score a "ten" in gymnastics. When she returned to her home in Romania, she immediately became embroiled in political turmoil because the repressive government would not give any kind of concessions to her as she tried to build a life around gymnastic exhibitionism. She had to leave the country and her life was very difficult. Finally, she was able to put her life together in this country.

Olga Korbut, also a gymnast, fell off the bar in Olympic competition. This was a dark moment for her, and everyone said that this would ruin her career. However, the next day she returned to win two gold medals.

Life demands as much courage and hopeful waiting from us as it does from the Olympic athletes. Life is a challenge of Olympic proportions demanding courage. Most of us express our courage in ways that are not in the spotlight; for example, the family who receives the word of cancer in a loved one and finds the courage to go through the "valley of the shadow," or families who are going through devastating infidelity, and know humiliation and insecurity but manage to know that they do not stand alone. God does not grow weary. A rebellious teenager, the death of a spouse, or deadly depression presents an unwanted opportunity to "wait and hope" for the strength of the Lord to uphold and renew our courage. Life demands Olympic courage from each of us at different points in our lives.

These encouraging words of Isaiah to God's people can be ours for living in these difficult days. In verse 28 he assures the people that God has power, and in the twenty-ninth verse he says that God gives power to the faint and weary. God *has* power and he *gives* power. Then in the next verse he says that we're wrong if we think that power is with the young — those who live under their own power break down. *Nobody* can make it under his own power. The challenges, hurdles, the weights and bars that we have to walk across like the gymnasts are too tough for us to do alone. It is the clear message of the Bible that human beings cannot make it through life under our own power. Even the youth will grow weary and the young (people) will utterly fall.

Isaiah then moves into a rhapsody about waiting hopefully on the Lord. This is the same kind of waiting that occurs while a mother waits on a baby to be born. Or like the farmer who has planted and is now waiting for the harvest. It is the same idea we find in Galatians when Paul says, "In the fullness of time [when time was pregnant], Jesus came." It is a purposeful waiting. The root word means *string, rope,* or *cord.* So we are to hold on to the rope during these waiting times, knowing that the answer of God is coming. The writer of Ecclesiastes very wisely said that there is a right time for everything. God, in his time, will take care of it. Then he says, "While you wait, you appropriate the future." The future response and answer becomes strength for life now. Faith is not a means by which you achieve victory but *living* by faith, hopeful waiting, is the victory itself. Victory is achieved when we understand God's timing and live with hopeful waiting.

Do you ever get up in the morning, look at your calendar and know the wind is in your face even before you put on your shoes? Do you feel like you are running through life? Do you think, "I'm tired; my soul is tired." Isaiah says that we will run and not grow weary when we go through life with God's strength.

The last part of verse 31 says: "They will run and not get tired, they will walk and not get weary." This is an important placement of words. We would probably have said that the phrase should be "walk, run, soar." But instead he said, "Soar, run, walk." All of us soar occasionally. It's the feeling you had when you asked her to marry you and she said yes. Or when you found out a new baby was coming; when you got a great new job; or when your child was accepted at his or her college of choice. We soar at moments like that. But we can't live with soaring all the time. Most of us can run, but we get tired. The "walk and not faint" is where most of us find ourselves. Someone asked John Bailey, the great Scottish theologian, "What was the critical difference for Great Britain during World War II? How did Great Britain really win the war?" His response was that the war was won by the plain man at the watch, doing a superlative job in the midst of the bombing. Most of us do more walking than running or flying. I'm talking about plodding through life. It can't always be soaring and running; it is mostly plodding. That's the way life is.

I have found that church is that way. I would like for every Sunday to be like Easter Sunday, but it can't be that way. Some Sundays we soar, some we run, and some we just walk. But God is with us in the walking as well as in the running and the soaring.

What does this mean for my life and yours? Are you facing challenges of Olympic proportion? Are you coming down to the point in your life where there are challenges that you don't want to face? What do you do? First of all, you exchange your weakness for his strength. That is what our scripture for this Epiphany Sunday says. Our strength is not going to make it. The young people fall out, exhausted. But God has strength beyond our imagination, so we can exchange our weakness for his strength. Don't worry,

God is big enough to handle our circumstances. So we exchange weakness for strength and take one step at a time.

The second thing we need to do is wait hopefully. That puts us in the process, the rhythm of God which will bring peace.

When I was in seminary, a preacher older than Methuselah was talking to my class of young preachers. He began to unfold the providence of God in his life as the pastor of a country church. He had been a faithful man at the watch. He had run and not grown weary; he had not fainted as he plodded along. Suddenly I realized that there really is a providence of God in our lives. He does care for each of us and will exchange our weakness and weariness for his power to soar when we need, to run as we must, and to walk all the time.

Peter Ueberroth was in charge of the 1984 Olympics in Los Angeles. Someone asked him about the defining moment in the Olympics for him. They expected him to relate a story of a great athlete with sinewy muscles and years of training. But Peter Ueberroth said that the most defining moment for him came in the torch relay across the United States. People from all walks of life are selected to carry the torch and every town sees it as a major event.

According to Ueberroth, the torch went through a small, wind-swept village in the western part of the United States. It was almost a ghost town with just a few stores for the local farmers and ranchers. This was the biggest thing that had ever happened in that town. The citizens wanted to find a way to choose the most representative person, so they decided that all the names of the townspeople would be placed in a hat, the mayor would draw a name, and that person would carry the torch. The mayor drew the name of a little girl, Amy, who had been physically challenged all her life. She could walk but not very well. She could take only a step or two before she would have to sit down. Her family had done everything possible for her, but she was confined to a wheelchair most of the time. For all practical purposes, Amy could never walk more than just a step or two. The selection committee didn't know what to do. They couldn't bear to tell Amy that she couldn't carry the torch. That would crush her. So the word in town was just to ignore the event. Maybe they had made too big a deal out of it, anyway. So the great day came and the mayor was there with just a few people. Amy, dressed in white shorts and t-shirt, was there with her family. National television cameras were there, but only a few townspeople were present. Amy was handed the torch. She got out of her chair and took one step. Everybody gasped. Then she took another step. Another gasp. Another step, then another, and another. It took about thirty seconds before the national news commentators realized what was happening. The tone of their voices and their enthusiasm for Amy went through the national television media and the people of the village at home, watching their television sets, realized that heroic history was being made in their little town. They came from their homes, ranches, and farms and almost instantly the street was lined with people who had come to see Amy carry the torch. Little Amy, with both hands on the torch, took it one step at a time. The people started chanting, "Amy, Amy," with each step until a crescendo went up in the village, "A—my, A—my, A—my," one step at a time until she stepped across the line and handed over the torch.

Only you know what burden you are carrying. Why not exchange your weakness for his strength? Wait for the pregnant will of God to give birth in your circumstance. Receive the gift of wings and legs and of endurance. One step begins it.

■ September 2007

Our Daily Bread®

For Personal and Family Devotions   *Since 1956*

WRITERS:
J. David Branon • Anne M. Cetas • William E. Crowder
Martin R. De Haan II • H. Dennis Fisher • Vernon C. Grounds
Cindy Hess Kasper • Julie Ackerman Link • David C. McCasland
David H. Roper • Joseph M. Stowell • Marvin L. Williams

INSIGHTS:
William E. Crowder • H. Dennis Fisher • Sim Kay Tee

ACKNOWLEDGMENTS:
Cover Photo: © Alex Soh
Sunrise, Kodanadu View Point, India

Poem: September 5 by C. Austin Miles
© Renewal 1940 The Rodeheaver Co.

MANAGING EDITOR: Tim Gustafson • SENIOR EDITOR: Clair Hess
EDITORS: Anne Cetas, Dennis De Haan, Alyson Kieda, David Sper
EDITORIAL ASSISTANT: Becky Knapp

REFUSING HELP

READ:
2 Kings 5:9-14

The manifestation of the Spirit is given to each one for the profit of all. —1 Corinthians 12:7

THE BIBLE IN ONE YEAR:
- Psalms 135–136
- 1 Corinthians 12

In 1869, John Roebling dreamed of building a massive bridge over the East River from Brooklyn to Manhattan. Unfortunately, at the outset of the project, his foot was crushed in an accident. In the recovery process, Roebling insisted he knew best and took charge of his own medical care. After refusing help, he began to show signs of tetanus. Before long, Roebling's jaw had locked into a permanent smile. Seizures and dementia plagued him until his death weeks later.

The Bible records a story about an independent person who balked at the help offered him. Naaman, a great warrior of Syria, suffered from leprosy. He sought out the prophet Elisha for healing but had preconceived ideas about how the healing should take place. So when Elisha sent his messenger to tell him to dip in the Jordan River seven times, Naaman was enraged. But Naaman's own servants gave wise advice: "If the prophet had told you to do something great, would you not have done it?" (2 Kings 5:13). And so Naaman followed the prophet's simple instructions, and his leprosy was cured.

God gives us gifts to aid each other (1 Cor. 12:7). But self-sufficiency shuts the door on much-needed help. Let's be open to the helping hand He provides. —Dennis Fisher

The Lord extends His gracious hand
To those in desperate need,
He lifts them up, He helps them stand
Through caring saints and loving deed. —D. De Haan

The first step in getting help is humility.

Seven Habits Of
Highly Effective Christians

2 Kings 5:1-14

Naaman was a mighty man of valor, but he was a leper. What a shock it must have been to this great man, the leader of the Syrian army, when the unaccountable lethargy and the terrible pain in the joints attacked his body. Then he discovered, especially on his back, the discolored patches and on them the little nodules which were pink at first and then turned brown. He knew that he had it, the dreaded leprosy. It was the scourge of the ancient world — the AIDS of his day. In crystal clear and cryptic language the Bible says it all. He had leprosy, that terrible skin disease that was dreaded not only because of the physical suffering involved but also because to have it meant one would be socially isolated.

Leprosy was very democratic. It infected the rich and the poor, the wise and the unwise, the powerful as well as the weak. Lepers were ritually unclean and thus isolated from the holy things. Interestingly enough, the Hebrew word for leprosy, *tsar-a'ath*, is generic and covers a full range of skin diseases from a mole to psoriasis.

The Bible makes it clear that Naaman was powerful and was afflicted with a terrible disease, and even the powerful man was helpless before the disease. A small microbe had rendered the great man powerless. He dreaded the outcome and the awful path the disease would take. The skin would become thick; the nodules would appear, especially in the face and the folds of the cheeks, nose, and forehead. The whole appearance of his face would change. Then the nodules would become larger and larger. Eventually they would ulcerate, and from them the foul discharge would come.

The eyebrows would fall out, the eyes would stare, the vocal cords would ulcerate, and the voice would become hoarse and the breath wheezing. Muscles would waste away, tendons contracting until the hands became like claws. After that would come progressive loss of fingers and toes, until in the end a whole hand or a whole foot would drop off. The duration of the disease would be anywhere from twenty to thirty years, the body dying, bit by bit. Naaman was a powerful man, but he was a leper. A small microbe stole the power of the man and in some ways of the Syrian army.

A little Israelite maid had been captured in a raid and found herself in the service of Naaman's wife. She told her mistress of the prophet of Israel. When the king of Syria heard of this, he encouraged Naaman to visit Israel to see the king and to be healed.

Naaman departed from Syria with much treasure, the price of his healing. It is not easy to figure accurately the rate of exchange between the gold and the silver reported in verse 5 and present currency. However, it is estimated by scholars that Naaman took a king's ransom, approximately $1,247,240, to Israel with him.[1]

The king was honest enough to admit he could not heal Naaman. However, he was reminded of the prophet Elisha and his miraculous powers, so he sent Naaman to him. Elisha bid Naaman to bathe seven times in the Jordan. Indignant, Naaman at first refused. The Jordan, a muddy river between two muddy banks, is not like the clean, pretty rivers of Syria. Finally, he agreed to do this as instructed, and was healed.

To how many of us do these words apply? They were mighty but were not whole or sound of soul. How many of us of strong intellect find an exalted position, financial power, and incredible influence, but have leprosy of the soul?

Consequently, our great abilities will bring no good to ourselves or to our world. Today we have proud and forceful people who ride high, achieve wealth and position, and yet are lepers. Some hidden moral defect cancels their real abilities and prevents them from attaining lives of positive influence and from commanding confidence and respect. They are mighty, but lepers.

This matter certainly applies to this sick culture of ours. Today's headlines of street riots and murder by mob violence, of corruption in high places of both government and business, of rampant commercialism, and of the rape of the environment give evidence to the leprosy in the soul of our culture. We are a great society of much potential, but we are halted by the leprosy of greed, savagery, and lust. We are mighty people but we are lepers.

Naaman traveled all the way from Syria to Israel to seek healing from the man of God named Elisha. Here we have the touchstone by which we may test the supremacy of our faith. It alone is able to purge our souls from the leprosy of sin. Only the religion that can do that can claim the final allegiance of the human heart. Naaman heard the prescription of Elisha, but he was indignant and felt that another river ought to do just as well. Are not Abana and Pharpar, rivers of Damascus, better than all the rivers of Israel? May I not wash in them and be clean? And so we prefer our substitutes. But substitutes are not good enough. Only the real thing will heal us today.

First of all, Naaman learned that the treasure he brought with him to Israel could not buy his health. "I cannot accept your money for that which I cannot do," said the king to Naaman. Money can do much, yet it has never purchased for anyone the healing of his soul nor the peace of his mind.

It is a good thing to have money and the things that money can buy. But it is a good thing to check up once in a while and make sure you have not lost the things that money cannot buy. We have reached the point in our culture where we believe that the dollar is a magic cure for our ills. We believe that if we have enough money, we can do anything or even build a great society.

I would not minimize the importance of money. I know it is food to eat, a roof over our heads, education for our children, books and music for the soul, medicine for the ill. Free speech, free press, free assembly, and free ballots — they are priceless but a poor makeshift for a man who lacks economic freedom. It is a good thing to have money and the things that money can buy, but is that the emphasis we must have? Some people possess much and own little. Other people possess little and own much. Possessing concerns things that can be bought and sold. Ownership concerns values that money cannot buy. Possession is having a house; ownership is having a home in it.

97

Every pastor knows people who would give anything to have happiness, peace of mind, and a good home. But it would do no good, for these things exist where money has no power. As soon as we learn that the dollar does not cure all our ills, we shall move along the road to true prosperity — peace and happiness.

(2) Also, Naaman learned that the secular forces could not deal with his issue. All his power and dignity were powerless in the face of his needs. The king of Israel, the seat of power, sent him to Elisha, the prophet of God.

We are learning that lesson today. Secular forces cannot heal our moral leprosy. In the long run, the law can get no more goodness out of the people than there is inside the people. The law and its force is much like a pump, and the water it pumps is the intellectual, moral, and spiritual life of the people, no better, no worse. As Woodrow Wilson told us, "Our nation cannot survive materially unless it is redeemed spiritually." This generation stands on the verge of an era that may see the death of our civilization — not so much from atomic bombs but in the spirit of people. A civilization always dies first at the roots. It dies in the death of all the forces that make people good, loyal, right, and strong within. Civilizations die as they are born, not with waving of flags or the noise of machine guns in the streets, but in the dark, in the stillness, when no one is aware of it. It never gets in the paper, but long afterward a few people looking back begin to see that it has happened. Sometimes in the stillness of the night, thinking of what is going on in our country, in our homes, and in places of entertainment, I wonder if that is not happening to us. If our nation is to survive, if her people are to be the individuals they ought to be, it will take more than the force of law to save it. It will take a profound moral and spiritual revival.

(3) The story also suggests that Naaman would rather have been cleansed a different way. He preferred a substitute for the Jordan. He preferred something more spectacular done by the holy man. In fact, he was indignant about the prophet's prescription. Elisha said it was this way or no way. Many of our people are in the same mood as Naaman. Modern prophets are telling them that secular

forces of inspiration and reform never healed them of their leprosy. They must wash "in the old river Jordan," and find their healing in the church and in Sunday Bible study and prayer, but the modern mind rebels. We want a surface cleansing; we don't want to change our souls. In the words of Thoreau, "For every thousand hacking at the leaves of evil, there is one striking at the root."[2] We can only achieve quantum improvements in our lives as we quit hacking at the leaves of attitude and behavior and get to work on the roots, the understandings from which our attitudes and behaviors flow.[3] We too must wash in the old river Jordan. We affirm that washing in church, in Sunday Bible study, and in prayer, but we don't like it.

Naaman was told to wash seven times in the river Jordan. No one really knows why it was seven times, although seven is the perfect and sacred number. Allow me to suggest seven things that will not only change a life at the core but also will make that life very stable and effective in a most difficult world.

1. We must make a profession of our faith in Jesus Christ as Savior and Lord.
2. We need to be baptized and affiliated with a local congregation.
3. We must study the Bible with a responsible church group, consistently, week after week.
4. We must pray and maintain a daily quiet time of introspection and meditation.
5. We must attend and participate in public worship on a regular basis with a community of faith to whom we have committed ourselves.
6. We must be good stewards of our income through the local congregation (I would be so bold as to recommend that we heed the biblical admonition to tithe).
7. This newly cleansed person should become engaged in personal acts of ministry.

These seven habits will make this new life effective. The act of contrition to be washed in the old muddy Jordan, not once but seven times, heals a life and sets it on a new course.

A soldier in the Second World War serving in the South Pacific wrote a letter to his father, who had been an alcoholic. The father knew the moral law, but he had not had the strength to fulfill it. Then he came in touch with God and found a power that the law, affluence, and success did not possess. The father bathed himself in the Jordan seven times. The son came home for a visit after his father's amazing transformation and, returning to the Pacific, he wrote this to him: "When I look back at how you changed, Pop, it seems like something from a fairy tale. All the fellows think they have the best father in the whole world. You've always been the best father to me. But now there is something else. I'm so proud of you, Pop, for what you've done in the past few years — it's better than being Lincoln's son or even Uncle Sam's son. You did wonderful things for other people too, but you have climbed the biggest barrier in humanity. You have conquered yourself. It takes a thousand men's wills and a million men's patience to do that completely. I started to tell you how I felt when I was home but I never got through the first sentence. I'll still never be able to put into words how much I love you for what you've done for Mom, me and the family."[4]

Only washing in the old Jordan can do that.

---

1. Russell Dilday, *Communicator's Commentary,* Vol. 9, p. 307.

2. Stephen Covey, *Seven Habits of Highly Effective People* (New York: Fireside Books, Simon & Schuster, 1989), p. 30.

3. Covey, p. 31.

4. From unpublished material shared with me by Dr. J. Chalmers Holmes.

Forever Plaid

Isaiah 43:18-25

A few years ago there was a popular off-Broadway musical which gave a good insight into how life was in the 1950s. The name of the show was *Forever Plaid,* which was the name of a singing group of four good guys (Sparky, Smudge, Jinx, and Frankie). They wore dinner jackets and bow ties and each vocal arrangement soared to stratospheric heights of harmony. They were the most sought after entertainment for weddings, conventions, proms, and country club socials, but they had bigger plans that included a zoom into the big-time entertainment world of Ed Sullivan or the *Perry Como Show.* But the musical taste of the country was changing and their kind of music didn't jive with the new wave of rock 'n' roll that was sweeping teenage Americans off their feet and into record stores.

Well, Forever Plaid landed their first big gig at the Airport Hilton Cocktail Bar, and en route to pick up their custom-made plaid tuxedos, they were slammed broadside by a school bus filled with eager teenagers who were on their way to witness the Beatles make their U.S. television debut on the *Ed Sullivan Show.* Miraculously, the teens all escaped injury but the members of Forever Plaid were killed instantly. Through some quirky power of harmony and expanding holes in the ozone layer, they are allowed to come back to perform the show and record the album they always dreamed of making.

This is a metaphor of our day. Because they were caught in a paradigm shift, the Plaids remained lost, not able to find a place to perform. It is like a visitor to Atlanta being given a map of downtown

Miami and sent out to find his way. A map of Miami will not fit the streets of Atlanta. This happens frequently in our world. A road or street map is supposed to tell us where we are and how to get where we're going. When the paradigm shifts, we're lost.

A paradigm is a model, a mold, or a standard by which one can be sure that he/she is on the right track. It is an accepted premise of life. Then suddenly everything changes. The city is full of new streets that are not yet on the map. You may have known your way around very well, but now there are new roads to travel and you don't know which way to go. The world believed that the universe rotated around the earth, but Galileo proved that to be incorrect. The paradigm shifted.

There was a time not long ago when the Swiss watchmakers made over 65 percent of the world's watches and eighty percent of the profits. Then one of the Swiss watchmakers discovered the quartz movement and tried to get the Swiss to adapt to it. They would not hear of it because who ever heard of a watch without a mainspring? In 1968 the Japanese picked up the new idea of the quartz watch at a show in Neuchatel, and you know what has happened. Japan now makes eighty percent of the world's watches and the Swiss are far behind. They were not open to new ideas and the paradigm had shifted.

A paradigm, or how we perceive reality, acts as a filter. It sets boundaries and rules and regulations that keep us from successfully anticipating the future. When the paradigm shifts, we are lost. We experience that feeling of trying to find our way in Atlanta with a street map of Miami — it just won't fit. When a paradigm has shifted, everyone goes back to zero. Yesterday's success is of no avail. Many times a successful past will block our vision of the future. You can be great under the old paradigm, but it does not count in the new. Everyone starts over.

Now the prophet in our text admonishes Israel to forget the "former things" (v. 18). Turn your attention instead to a *new* thing. *Former things* refer to the events surrounding the first exodus; the *new* thing is the inspiration of Israel from exile and the transformation of the wilderness into a paradise. The prophet means by his admonition that the wonders of the new exodus will be such as this new exodus, and this *new* thing which God is going to do will be such as to cause the first exodus to pale into significance by comparison.

God is continually doing a *new* thing for his people, but his people are continually looking for *former things*. What does this mean for us? The shifting paradigms do affect the church. You may note that in Joel 2:25 it is stated that "I will make up to you for the years that the swarming locust has eaten..." meaning that the years have taken their toll on God's work in the world and he will make it right. He will make up for it. We see this actually taking place at Pentecost when the church was born. Peter is saying, "This is that." He means that what you learned from the Old Testament scriptures is now being fulfilled before your eyes. The church has been born; Pentecost is here; the old religious system is dead. At Pentecost three thousand were added to the Kingdom of God and thus began a new paradigm. The old paradigm was left behind and a new paradigm opened.

The greatest illustration of what happens to an institution or person who is not open to changing with the new paradigm is the Jerusalem church. They absolutely refused to allow change. The church fathers insisted that all the old rules be followed, no matter what. They were like so many church members today — "It is more important to follow the church constitution and bylaws than it is to win people to the Kingdom of God." Every church has enough of those to keep the body from doing God's task on earth — winning the world to Christ. Play by the rules and let the rest of the world go to hell, literally. The Jerusalem church was plagued with these Judaizers who insisted on the old paradigm even while the new paradigm was right before them.

The opposite of this was the church at Antioch. As you know, the disciples were first called Christians in Antioch and the church in that city was the cradle of Christianity and the Christian missionary movement. This church, by virtue of accepting and acting on the new paradigm, has become the model for all time of witnessing and reaching out to all the world. The Jerusalem Conference, well known to New Testament scholars, was called to decide which way it would be. The Jerusalem church wanted to stay with the old paradigm and so they turned inward and died. The new paradigm was gladly accepted by the Antioch church and they grew and became the missionary standard by which we are all measured to this day. Will it be the old way or the new way?

Now, what about us? What about our church? We fared well in the '50s and '60s under the old system. We "did church" really well in those days. But now, times have changed. The old paradigm has shifted and we have to be like the great church at Antioch. We must turn loose the old ways and grasp the new. It is impossible to hold on to the past while facing the future. This does not mean that we are changing our belief structure. That is firm and secure. This is the church of the Lord Jesus Christ and we are here to do his work. But we have a new map now, a new paradigm, and we must not get lost by reading the old map. It is always a temptation to go back to the old ways and be controlled by people of the old paradigm.

I know some churches that have become frozen in the nineteenth century and they only want the glory days back. They keep thinking that if they do their work the old way happy days will follow. Perhaps if the church could once again have a great pulpit orator like Dr. Hadden Bensober, the glory would again return. This cannot be done. The paradigm has shifted and there is no way to go back. The way back is death. Like Israel in the wilderness, we long for the safety and certainty of Egypt, the *former thing*. We want the "good old days" to return. Our cities are full of churches that are controlled by people in the old paradigm. Our empty pews are a testimony to the fact that the old days will not return. It is so sad to see a once vital, vibrant church turn inward and die.

When my family and I were in London in 1969, I was determined to worship in Spurgeon's Tabernacle. In the days when Spurgeon was preaching there, the church was alive and jammed with people (more than 6,000) at every service. We got a taxi to take us to the Tabernacle on Sunday morning, and as we walked up the great front steps, we had to dodge the pigeons and walk through a lot of dirt. Inside, there were a few people scattered around (not more than a hundred) but no one ever greeted us. It was a sad ending to a once vital church. The paradigm shifted, but they had not figured it out. It is true that often a successful past will block our vision of the future.

What shall we do? There is no going back. A pastor may find a quiet church where he can do ministry — perform rituals, conduct weddings, attend rehearsal dinners, keep traditions, but he/she won't like it. It is impossible to go back to Egypt as the Israelites begged to do. We are not called to safety, nor are we on a career track. This is an adventure. We have to go forward. We cannot be like the Jerusalem church and turn inward. The good old days are gone and they aren't coming back. Luther at Worms, the Wesleyan revivals, the Haystack prayer meetings, Spurgeon's Tabernacle — they're all gone. They are the old paradigm and we are the new.

It is important that we not take ourselves too seriously. Yes, we take the gospel and the church seriously, but remember what Bonhoffer wrote on his cell wall in a Nazi prison, "It will all be over in a hundred years." You recall that General Patton was afraid the war would be over and he would not be in it. That's the way we should be. This is life — now — we must live it!

God is still in control and the church is worth the effort. God gave us the freedom to be who he wants us to be. He died for the church and that freedom.

Don't color me plaid. I'm shifting with the paradigm. How about you? And don't forget to "dance like no one is looking and sing like you're being paid!"

Failure Is
Not Final

Hosea 2:14-20

We are offered wonderful news from the Bible on this eighth Sunday of Epiphany. God has a way of bringing us the very personal lives of his chosen people. We are God's chosen whether we fit the profile of the clergy or as laity — or, as my family would say, normal people. The story told in Hosea is one of great personal pain and suffering and brokenheartedness on the part of this prophet of God. His beloved wife Gomer leaves his home and hearth for a life of infidelity. She pursues other lovers but soon presents a picture of frustration and despair as she is disposed of by her uncommitted lovers. However, though she chose to leave Hosea's home, he never let her out of his heart. He yearned for her and passionately sought to find her and return her to the family with tender, loving kindness and affection.

This story of the tenderness and devotion of Hosea searching and finding Gomer is used by God to demonstrate how he loves his people who have "played the harlot" with his heart and devotion. Israel found themselves in a wilderness, the valley of Achor, which became known as the door of hope. Out of the failure of Israel to be faithful and committed to God, he provided a door of hope — a way out of their failure and despair.

The Lord, in speaking to Hosea, reached back into the history of Israel to show him that he, the Lord, was still in control. He reminded Hosea of the scene of great destruction and pathos of which we can read in Joshua 7 and 8. The story is one of the disobedience of the family of Achan and the consequences of their greed and sin. Joshua and the children of Israel were praising God and reveling in the victory of the battle of Jericho. Now it was time to push forward to capture the town of Ai. Spies from Israel reported to Joshua that Ai would be so easy to take that there was no need for a full army to be sent to battle. So a detachment was sent forth to capture Ai, but they were defeated and had to flee from the men of Ai.

Needless to say, this was a humiliating turn of events. Joshua tore his clothes and fell to the earth on his face before the ark of the Lord, wailing and questioning God's leadership. God was quick to let Joshua know that Israel was experiencing the logical consequences of sin and transgression and gave instructions on how to deal with this situation. It would not be a pretty sight. It turned out that Achan was the culprit, and he and his family and all that belonged to him plus the stolen property were taken out to the valley. There they were stoned to death and burned, and to this day the name of the place is called the Valley of Achor (trouble).

What is significant about this story, however, is that immediately the Lord turned from his burning anger and used this valley of trouble to show Israel how he, the Lord, could provide hope and victory to those who are committed to him and obey his guidance through all things. God gave explicit instructions as to how the battle against Ai was to be fought, and they obeyed. This time there was resounding victory. So the valley of Achor (trouble) became the door of hope.

How many of us have felt locked in a valley of grief and despair? Is that where you are now? No one is free of disasters, of failures that may or may not be of our own making. Today you must hear the word of God to you: failure is not final. There is a door of hope wherever you are in the valley. This valley of Achor is the door of hope for everyone who longs for the tenderness of the Father's love.

One of my favorite stories of failure not being final is the one about Babe Ruth, the home-run champion of the world. The other part of that story is that he also led in strikeouts! Thank goodness there is no award for strikeout champion. Babe Ruth said, "Anybody can get on base. I don't want to spend my life just being on base, so I go for the center field fence." And so he struck out occasionally!

Bernie Marcus was an executive with Handy Man stores, but one day corporate headquarters was displeased with earnings and fired Bernie. He didn't know what to do. He felt like a complete failure. That was for him the valley of Achor. Then some friends pointed him to the door of hope, and they began a new concept in the hardware business called "Home Depot." Everybody laughed at the idea, including a dear friend of mine who was in the hardware business. "It'll never amount to anything," was his verdict. Well, we all know the success story of Home Depot. Bernie Marcus decided that *failure is not final.*

The biggest failure in corporate history since the Edsel is New Coke. Sergio Zyman was the man who had been a sterling performer at the Coca-Cola Company. He had introduced Diet Coke, and it was an overnight success with stock prices soaring. Then Sergio Zyman went to the corporation and said, "I used to work with Pepsi and they had assessed the taste values of the younger generation, and we need to reformulate Coke's taste." They agreed and called it New Coke. This new product was launched with great excitement and fanfare. But everyone who tasted it said, "This is awful, the worst stuff we've ever tasted." How would you like to have your whole career riding on a can of New Coke? He was a hero no longer. He became their scapegoat. New Coke was taken off the market and the old Coke was reintroduced as Classic Coke. Sergio Zyman went away to do some consulting for a while. He was trudging through his valley of Achor. Classic Coke came back stronger than it had ever been before, and that year became the best year in Coca-Cola's history up to that point. Officials at Coca-Cola said, "We wish we could have a New Coke debacle every ten years. It would do wonders for our company." Now Zyman has been rehired by Coke and he has a fine executive position. He is considered a hero and not the butt of jokes. He found the door of hope in his valley of Achor. *Failure is not final!*

Many of the disciples whom Jesus chose were not known for their successful lives. For example, Levi (Matthew) was lumped right in there with sinners and tax collectors (Mark 2:13-22). He was not the most respected man in the community. In fact, Matthew was a well-hated man. Even as Matthew was sitting at the tax collectors' table, his heart must have been aching. He must have heard about Jesus and tried to catch a glimpse of him as he passed by. He probably even tried to slip into the group following Jesus to hear what he had to say. Matthew was really like a man without a country because he had sold out to Rome, but they considered him good only to collect taxes, and the Jews hated him with a passion and had nothing but scorn for him. His self-esteem had hit rock bottom and he hated himself for what he had become. He knew he was a failure — to himself, to his people — and he ached for restoration. His valley of Achor seemed to have no door of hope until Jesus walked by and opened it wide. Matthew did not hesitate a moment, but got up from his changing table, left all the papers and money on the table, and followed Jesus. When the door of hope opened, he bolted through it. Here was his chance to put his failures behind him and get on with life in Christ. *Failure is not final!*

The disciple who probably had the brightest and most promising beginning was Simon Peter. He was smart and quick-witted, devoted to Jesus, and seemingly fearless in the face of trouble. His star was ascending and burning brightly. He seemed to know all the right answers, and then his eclipse began. It was only partial, at first, almost immediately following one of Peter's brilliant confessions that "Thou are the Christ, the Son of the Living God." He had been praised for that statement and he was feeling good about himself. Then Jesus began to tell his followers about the days and events to come — all very distasteful — and Peter took his first steps into the valley of Achor (Matthew 16:16, 21-23). He heard words coming at him from Jesus that cut like a whip across his face. All who heard it were shocked: "Out of my way, Satan!"

But wait, Peter was to walk still deeper into the valley of Achor. Failure was stalking him, demoralizing and crippling him. Yes, there were glimpses of hope; Peter was present at the transfiguration (Matthew 17:1-9), and suggested that they stay there. (He probably felt safe there.) Peter was also present with Jesus in Gethsemane along with James and John, but none of them could stay awake to be with Jesus as he agonized in prayer. The door of hope was cracked, but Peter could not push it open. And now, as Caiaphas and the high priests ridiculed and humiliated Jesus, Peter was hanging around the edges, following at a distance. Then Peter seemed to lunge into the depth of the valley of Achor. Suddenly, he heard the cock crow three times and he remembered what Jesus had said, and he went out and wept bitterly. The worst had happened. He had denied his Lord. Is your valley of Achor filled with regrets — "Why did I do that, or say that?"; "How could I have been so stupid?"; "If only I had...." Is your valley choked with words you'd like to recall or shameful attitudes? Well, it seems that we're all in good company, but we can take heart. There is a door of hope at the end of the valley. The door of Resurrection! The women who went to the tomb to minister to Jesus found the stone rolled away. Angels who were there told them that Jesus was risen and to go tell his disciples *and Peter!* Can you imagine the heartstopping joy they all experienced? But none so much as Peter. *Failure is not final!*

Later Jesus appeared to Simon Peter and asked him three times, "Do you love me?" It grieved Peter that Jesus needed so much reassurance. Perhaps it was the parallel to Peter's three denials. Then fifty days later Simon Peter was at Pentecost and preached with such power from God that the church was formed and three thousand people were saved that day. A new day was inaugurated in this world — *failure is not final!* The valley of Achor has become the door of hope.

A film clip from the movie *Dead Man Walking*, starring Susan Sarandon and Sean Penn, features a scene in which Sean Penn, surrounded by some crusty old prison guards, is being taken from his cell to the execution chamber. One of the guards calls out, "Dead man walking." That is the way a lot of people live. They are dead men/women walking because they have determined that their failure is final. Haven't you been around people who just seem to be losers? It's because they have decided that they are failures — in marriage, career, church relationships — life in general. They act as if they had a great big "F" (for failure) on their forehead instead of a great big "H" for the door of hope.

Failures are people who won't take a risk, won't even try. The Bible strongly admonishes people to take a risk: don't just stand

111

there wringing your hands, *do something*, even if it is wrong. Jesus said, "Because you are neither hot nor cold I will spew thee out of my mouth," to the church at Laodicea. Sometimes we make bad decisions, choices that are not the best, but the Bible only condemns those who do not try.

Failure is not final unless you want it to be. *Failure is not final* because God doesn't want it to be. We need to go through the issues in our own lives and determine how we are engaging ourselves in life. I believe in heaven and hell. But I have found another chapter of hell right here. Do you know who the most miserable people are? Not the ones who have tried and failed. The most miserable people I know are those who never decide. They are living in hell every day. They can't make up their minds. They can see both sides; they keep all their options open, but they never want to close off an avenue or an option. There comes a time you have to choose. You can't live life always having your options open. You are living in an indecision hell. And your life goes down as mediocre, unhappy. You have made no mistakes; there is no scar tissue; there is no manure in your barn. When you die, you are gone. Nobody remembers you for the good things or the bad things, and while you are here, you drive everybody crazy because you are caught in the hell of indecision.

When I first came to Atlanta, the dean of the Textile School at Georgia Tech was in our church, and he asked if I would like to meet Coach Bobby Dodd. Of course, I wanted to meet him; any red-blooded American boy wants to meet a legendary coach who has won impossible football games. So the dean and I went out to Rose Bowl Field to meet Coach Dodd. It was a great day. This tall, lanky Tennessean said, "Do you know why we call this Rose Bowl Field? We bought this field with the money that Georgia Tech made when they played in the 1928 Rose Bowl, and I never let the boys forget it." When we got in the car to go home after the conversation, the dean turned to me and asked if I knew the significance of the coach's statement. Then he told me the most amazing story.

In 1928 Georgia Tech went out to California to play the University of California in the Rose Bowl. It was a big deal then, and it would be a big deal today. The first half of the football game was as tight as it could be — both teams struggling in the middle of the field; neither team could do anything. They came down to the final minutes of the first half and Georgia Tech fumbled. In those days the rules allowed you to pick up a fumble and run with it. So the opposing team, the University of California, picked up the fumble. The boy ran 68 yards the wrong way. He was tackled by his own man just a few feet from his own goal. He had almost scored a touchdown for Georgia Tech. His name, Roy Reigals, is legendary now. There were a few more seconds to play. Tech pushed them back over the goal and scored two points, and those two points were the margin of victory in that game. The half was over, and they went to the locker room. Coach Nibs Price of the University of California looked at his boys, and knew they were disillusioned about what had happened. Roy Reigals went over to a corner, wrapped a blanket around himself, and sobbed during the whole halftime. The coaches did what was normally done by coaches during the halftime, getting the players ready to go back on the field. Then he turned to the team and said, "The team that started the first half is going to start the second." The boys got up, ran down the tunnel and out onto the field to start the second half of the Rose Bowl, except for Roy Reigals. He sat in the corner with a blanket around him, sobbing. The coach went over to him and said, "Roy, I said that the team that started the first half will start the second." Roy said, "I can't go out there. I've embarrassed you. I've embarrassed the team. I've embarrassed the University of California, and my family. Everyone connected with me at all has been embarrassed by this horrible thing I've done. I will not play any more football ever." Coach Nibs Price looked at him and said, "Roy, I said to you that the team that started the first half will start the second." Finally, Roy Reigals understood what he was talking about, pulled himself together, ran down the tunnel, and joined the team. Sports historians tell us that nobody ever played a better half of football than Roy Reigals in the 1928 Rose Bowl. *The team that started the first half will start the second.*

Hear me. If the Bible has anything to say, it is clear — *failure is not final. Failure is not final.* God loves you in your valley of

113

Achor enough to provide the door of hope. God loves you with your scars, because of your scars. The Lord we serve has scars. *Failure is not final.*

Transfiguration Of Our Lord
(Last Sunday After The Epiphany)

No Shortcut
To Glory

2 Kings 2:1-12

At the beginning of every new fall term, Dr. Sydnor Staley, the first president of Southeastern Theological Seminary at Wake Forest, North Carolina, welcomed the new freshman class with these words: "I wish that we could give each of you a theological diploma today. Then those who desire an education could go about their studies unhindered by those who are spiritually shallow."

The student experience in a theological seminary is interesting as well as educational. There are all kinds of people there for a variety of reasons. Most seminaries have a way to screen applicants so that there is some consistency in the purpose of the student body, but many do not last even the full first year. Some are not prepared for the difficult studies. They come expecting instant recognition of their spirituality and become weary of the work and interaction with those who do not agree with them. I heard of an incident where one student in particular was so impressed with his own insights that he couldn't understand why he was not given an immediate degree and sent on his way. His fellow students found an advertisement in a religious journal selling a theological diploma for 25 dollars and a Doctorate in Theology for a mere fifty dollars. They all pitched in and ordered the Doctorate in Theology for their friend and had a grand presentation party.

The truth is that we all wish to have a shortcut to spirituality. Our world is full of disposable and instant everything, so it seems only logical that there would be some way to mix water with some substance, pop it in the ecclesiastical microwave, and produce a warm, fuzzy religious experience. We want the wonder and glory of religious experience served to us on a silver platter (as long as we don't have to polish the silver!). We would like to bask in the glory of a religious experience comparable to that which Peter, James, and John enjoyed at the transfiguration of Jesus. They witnessed Jesus talking to Moses and Elijah and saw that there was a supernatural change in Jesus. It was a glorified manifestation of the greatness of Jesus and served as a preparation for the events that were coming soon — Jerusalem and the cross. However, they were not allowed to linger here. This overpowering religious experience was for a purpose. It was to allow these disciples to understand that Jesus had a mission from God and that this was helping to prepare Jesus himself for the difficult events to come.

In the Gospel of Mark this transfiguration scene is one of recognition, the moment in which the reader and a chosen few are permitted to see Jesus in full glory. As a cloud formed, overshadowing them, they heard a voice saying, "This is my beloved Son ... Listen to him!" (Mark 9:7). This is similar to the baptism of Jesus in that a voice from heaven identified Jesus as God's son. However, here the voice speaks to the disciples. This transfiguration also anticipates the resurrection, although there is no actual resurrection in Mark's Gospel. There is the appearance of Moses and Elijah, who had come to be associated with the Messianic Age in Judaism and Christianity. Being here with Jesus says that the anticipated messiah and the end-time prophecies are fulfilled in Jesus. They disappear, saying that the old is ended and the new has come. We note also that Jesus does not speak. Just as at the baptism, God acts and speaks concerning Jesus. We hunger for the wonder of a transfiguration experience, but are we ready to experience the journey to Jerusalem and the cross? This hunger for wonder is in the soul of our churches.

The truth is that we have developed all types of substitutes for authentic spiritual experience. We rally around political causes or divide into liberal, conservative, moderate, or fundamental camps. We become "liberal" Baptists or "high church" Lutherans or "low church" Catholics. We run to anything to give us some religious certainty and wonder. Perhaps we should develop contemporary

116

worship or high liturgy for worship — fads and instant religion — for quick-fix solutions for spiritual barrenness.

How does one encounter religious experience and certainty without resorting to fads and quick fixes and sham credentials? We long to go to the Mount of Transfiguration. Our souls thirst to have communion with mystery. We need more than Saturday soccer games and car-pooling. We deeply yearn to go beyond careers and 401Ks, bulletin boards, and business plans. As Peggy Lee sang, "Is that all there is?" We need more than this. To experience this mystery we must do hard labor and forget instant formulas and religious microwaves. We must be willing to depart from the god we created in our own image. We yearn for the Mount of Transfiguration and for Elijah, Moses, and Jesus, but we settle for the slough of despondency because we want instant experience.

Again, we ask the question: How does one encounter authentic spiritual experience? This is not easy to answer, but there are some clues in the Old Testament lecton for this day. We find it in the relationship of the old prophet Elijah and Elisha, his designated successor. Elijah was the greatest prophet of the northern kingdom from the ninth century B.C.E. and was from Tishbe in Gilead. He was direct, rough, abrupt, and perhaps the most romantic character that Israel produced. He performed miracles, struggled against Baalism, filled a prophetic role, and has been assigned an eschatological relationship to the messiah.

Near the end of his ministry, as he was resting in a cave while running away from Queen Jezebel after he had the prophets of Baal killed, the Lord appeared to him. Among the things that the Lord spoke to Elijah about were some instructions. He told Elijah to go back the way he came and go to the Desert of Damascus, and while there anoint Elisha, son of Shaphat, to succeed him as prophet. Elijah did this by throwing his cloak over Elisha's shoulders (1 Kings 19:19). This act denoted God's intention to bestow the prophetic powers upon him as the successor to the great Elijah. Our text focuses on the last days of Elijah's time on earth and what I believe to be Elijah's development and preparation of Elisha to receive the mantle.

117

He engaged the young prophet in three experiences to test him and prepare him for the forthcoming responsibilities. We first see the travel itinerary of Elijah and Elisha. Perhaps Elijah was giving Elisha a short historic tour of Israel before departing this world. They began their journey in Gilgal, where the Hebrews first made camp after crossing the Jordan River, and made their way to Bethel, which was a sacred temple site. From there they returned to Jericho (the Hebrews' first triumph west of the Jordan) and then made their way to the Jordan River (scene of the miraculous crossing). Finally, Elijah parts the water with his mantle and the two cross over. Elisha faithfully stayed with Elijah throughout this journey, even though Elijah offered him opportunities to stay behind. This is the second test that Elijah presented to Elisha, and he faithfully and steadfastly proved that he was a true follower. The third test resided in the "sons of prophets" who, in every location, warned Elisha that Elijah's departure was imminent. No one knew exactly where it would occur or the exact circumstances, but Elisha was steadfast. He would not be discouraged from loyally remaining with Elijah.

What about people today who want instant religion, who don't have staying power? We are not ready to experience or serve in any significant way until we make the journey from start to finish. Every pastor knows of people who, after some event in their lives, rush into their studies and profess to want to "get active and serve through my church." Most of us know they do not want to usher, feed hungry people, teach children in Sunday School, or build shelters for the homeless. They really have no intention to give a cup of cold water in Jesus' name. They do not wish to "take the towel." Their desire is to become the chairperson of the governing board, or in some other way "sit at the head table." They are like the rich young ruler, in that they do not wish to make any sacrifice. The kingdom should be glad to have them.

There is something that happens on the journey to prepare us for the mountain. Elijah told Elisha that if he could see his (Elijah's) departure, he would be qualified to receive the prophetic mantle. Eyes to see are absolutely necessary for the prophetic task — the days on the road from Gilgal to Bethel to the Jordan; actually living in close proximity with him and talking together, watching him interact with the "sons of the prophets" and the village people helped Elisha develop eyes to see.

Religious wonder and epiphany come in God's good time to those who have been on the way doing the tasks of the kingdom, not to the religious hotshots who show up without any commitment wanting to share in the glory. Perhaps the athletes are right — no pain, no gain.

Before the mantle would be given by Elijah, the persistent loyalty and fidelity of Elisha needed to be proven. Is he a true disciple or a "flash in the pan"? We see in 1 Kings 19:19-21 that Elisha demonstrated the characteristics of a true disciple. At first, he hesitated to follow Elijah, begging first to bid farewell to his family. Elijah said no, but Elisha immediately slaughtered his yoke of twelve oxen and offered them up as a feast for the people to show that he was forsaking his past and literally "burning his bridges behind him." Elisha had the opportunity to leave Elijah many times, but he steadfastly remained with him.

During the Revolutionary War, George Washington had an abundance of soldiers volunteer to fight during the summer months, but as winter came, with rations in short supply and blankets being scarce, they began to slip silently from camp and return to the warmth of their families. After some weeks of this, General Washington despaired of "summer soldiers," saying that he could not win a war with them.

The kingdom of God has had its problems with summer soldiers. The same people who travel every weekend want the church to be at its spiritual best when they do attend. Someone should work with the nursery and teach Sunday school, but "I must be away next week to attend a football game. And, by the way, God does not seem as real to me as he once did." In the parable of the lost sheep it is clear that the lost one was not stolen from the flock — he just gradually nibbled himself away. No prophetic mantle can fall on anyone whose faithfulness is that shallow and whose spiritual strength is that vacuous.

Many a young preacher wants to begin at the cathedral church on Easter Sunday. He does not want to preach in the jails and mission stations, lead youth groups, or visit hospitals and hospice centers. Elisha requested that he be given a double portion of the spirit of Elijah. This is not a request to exceed his mentor, but rather a request for the portion of the inheritance that would be given to the firstborn. After making the journey with Elijah, he still wanted to succeed his mentor and be the leader of the "sons of the prophets." It is interesting that as Elisha witnessed Elijah being taken up to heaven in a whirlwind, he called out, "My father! My father!" He truly felt that he was the son of the prophet.

A summer mission volunteer called her pastor from the inner-city ghetto where she was working. It was one of the rare evenings which she had to herself. She had been at her post for four weeks and was tired, spiritually and physically. When she told this to her pastor, she concluded by saying words to the effect, "I did not know what this work was like until I got here. The romance and glamour I had in my mind when I came is gone. I have homesickness and fatigue, loneliness and disappointment. I am much more realistic than before, but I still want to give myself to the task for the rest of my life because through all of this I see the hand of God in it." She had developed spiritual eyes. She had a transfiguration.

Eyes to see the invisible are developed along the way and are necessary to do his work. No one, lay or clergy, in one's right mind can endure *this* work if one does not have eyes to see.

Books In This Cycle B Series

GOSPEL SET
A God For This World
Sermons for Advent/Christmas/Epiphany
Maurice A. Fetty

The Culture Of Disbelief
Sermons For Lent/Easter
Donna E. Schaper

The Advocate
Sermons For Sundays After Pentecost (First Third)
Ron Lavin

Surviving In A Cordless World
Sermons For Sundays After Pentecost (Middle Third)
Lawrence H. Craig

Against The Grain — Words For A Politically Incorrect Church
Sermons For Sundays After Pentecost (Last Third)
Steven E. Albertin

FIRST LESSON SET
Defining Moments
Sermons For Advent/Christmas/Epiphany
William L. Self

From This Day Forward
Sermons For Lent/Easter
Paul W. Kummer

Out From The Ordinary
Sermons For Sundays After Pentecost (First Third)
Gary L. Carver

Wearing The Wind
Sermons For Sundays After Pentecost (Middle Third)
Stephen M. Crotts

Out Of The Whirlwind
Sermons For Sundays After Pentecost (Last Third)
John A. Stroman

SECOND LESSON SET
Humming Till The Music Returns
Sermons For Advent/Christmas/Epiphany
Wayne Brouwer

Ashes To Ascension
Sermons For Lent/Easter
John A. Stroman